T0294163

THE
PERFECT SCOUT

Above left: George W. Quimby, c. 1880s; photograph courtesy of Stephen Murphy.

Above right: Mary Stevenson Quimby, c. 1880s; photograph courtesy of Stephen Murphy.

The University of Alabama Press   Tuscaloosa

THE
PERFECT SCOUT

*A Soldier's Memoir of the Great March to the Sea
and the Campaign of the Carolinas*

GEORGE W. QUIMBY

EDITED BY ANNE SARAH RUBIN AND STEPHEN MURPHY

The University of Alabama Press
Tuscaloosa, Alabama 35487-0380
uapress.ua.edu

Copyright © 2018 by the University of Alabama Press
All rights reserved.

Inquiries about reproducing material from this work should be addressed
to the University of Alabama Press.

Typeface: Adobe Caslon
Cover image: Engraving of Union scouts on horseback,
from *Harper's Weekly*, 1864; courtesy of the Library of Congress
Cover design: Todd Lape / Lape Designs

Library of Congress Cataloging-in-Publication Data

Names: Quimby, George W., 1842–1926, author. |
Rubin, Anne S., editor.

Title: The perfect scout : a soldier's memoir of the great March to the
Sea and the campaign of the Carolinas / George W. Quimby ; edited by
Anne Sarah Rubin and Stephen Murphy.

Description: Tuscaloosa : The University of Alabama Press, [2018] |
Includes bibliographical references and index.

Identifiers: LCCN 2017023894| ISBN 9780817319717 (cloth) |
ISBN 9780817391614 (e book)

Subjects: LCSH: Quimby, George W., 1842–1926. | Soldiers—United
States—19th century—Biography. | Scouts (Reconnaissance)—United
States—19th century—Biography. | United States—History—Civil
War, 1861–1865—Personal narratives. | United States—History—Civil
War, 1861–1865—Scouts and scouting. | Sherman's March to the Sea. |
Sherman's March through the Carolinas. | United States—History—
Civil War, 1861–1865—Campaigns.

Classification: LCC E601 .Q69 2018 | DDC 973.7/8092 [B] —dc23

LC record available at https://lccn.loc.gov/2017023894

CONTENTS

PART I   The Great March to the Sea

PART II   The Campaign of the Carolinas

PREFACE

Stephen Murphy

My wife, Christopher Smith Murphy, is a great-great-granddaughter of George Quimby. Like many descendants of Civil War veterans, she has been to family reunions and heard stories about this common ancestor. The family had learned about his service in the Union Army: that he served under Sherman, was a scout, and possibly had written a book or books about his exploits. However, the only concrete mention of the book is in the 1926 *History of Whatcom County*, which includes a section about George Quimby. The author of the piece had apparently interviewed Quimby and mentions his book, along with many flattering comments about him: "Fidelity of purpose, keenness of perception, unswerving integrity and sound common sense have been the marked characteristics of his makeup, and these qualities, together with his genial and friendly manner, have won for him the sincere respect and esteem of all who know him." At the time the article was written, Quimby was eighty-four; he died later that year.

I discovered the manuscript in 1990 after my father-in-law passed away. It fell to me to clean out his house in Seattle—a process that took nine months and filled twenty-one Dumpsters. Amid his many collections, handiwork, and debris were three legal-sized folders containing George Quimby's neatly typed memoirs of his exploits in the Union Army. One, a short book that covers his first year when he was a private and was taken prisoner and escaped, may have been written at an earlier time because it lacks the style of the other two books. It is not included in this collection. Here is a brief passage from Quimby's first chapter: "Perhaps no other branch of the service enabled one to see the inside of secession and to become fairly well acquainted with the true feelings and general kindness of the individuals of the South, especially of the families and the old men and returned wounded soldiers. We gradually learned to respect, and then to sympathize with, them and finally would as soon thought of robbing our mother as those kind people of Georgia." What follows are Quimby's adventures as a scout under General Sherman in the last years of the war. Although in his introduction Quimby mentions he regrets he had only a few years of school, he obviously became educated, because except for minor editing for spelling and punctuation, the memoirs you are about to read are as he wrote them. They were probably written in the early 1900s, the time many half-century Civil War reunions were taking place, when he lived in Northwest Washington State. It is not clear who Nellie and Maude, the girls to whom he dedicates the book, are, but they likely are granddaughters living in the same area.

I have taken the liberty of retitling the manuscript, as it becomes a book, to *The Perfect Scout*. This better captures the spirit of Quimby's story and adventures.

INTRODUCTION

ANNE SARAH RUBIN

IN THE FALL OF 1869, at the fourth annual reunion of the Society of the Army of the Tennessee, Brigadier General Edward F. Noyes lauded Sherman's army. He recalled their successes at Vicksburg and Lookout Mountain, their campaign for Atlanta. Then he turned to the Great March to the Sea and through the Carolinas, recalling almost wistfully, that "in this rollicking picnic expedition there was just enough of fighting for variety, enough of hardship to give zest to the repose which followed it, and enough of ludicrous adventure to make its memory a constant source of gratification."[1] Noyes could well have been describing George W. Quimby's memoir, *The Perfect Scout*. Quimby's stories of drunken frolics and narrow escapes read like an adventure novel, but are all true. He gives a new twist to the familiar stories of the March, reminding readers that while the Union soldiers faced few full-scale battles, the campaign still could be dangerous.

Quimby's memoir is heavy on action and light on ideology. We never know what motivated him to enlist or how he felt about emancipation. We do see how he and his fellow scouts interacted with a range of Confederate civilians, and from his generally kind portraits, we can infer a sort of reunionist sentiment. Quimby appears to have written this around 1901, in the wake of the Spanish-American War, and he evinces no desire to settle old scores. Rather, his tone is that of a natural storyteller, keeping his audience occupied on the edge of their seats. That's also not to say that he embellishes; to the contrary, whenever possible he includes citations to other evidence to support his version of events.

Much of the value of Quimby's memoir comes in his having been a scout. For all that we know about Civil War soldiers, there are very few works focusing on individual scouts themselves.[2] Rather, most writings about Civil War espionage or intelligence tend toward the sensational, emphasizing dramatic incidents in the lives of well-known spies like the Pinkertons, Belle Boyd, Rose O'Neal Greenhow, Henry Young, or Timothy Snyder.

For example, Robert P. Broadwater's *Civil War Special Forces: The Elite and Distinct Fighting Units of the Union and Confederate Armies* devotes only one brief chapter to scouts and spies.[3] Edwin Fishel's *The Secret War for the Union* promises to tell "the untold story" of Civil War military intelligence, but does so from the relatively limited perspective of Virginia. Nevertheless, he does point out that often studies of intelligence are divorced from the study of battles and campaigns—there's little recognition of the influence of what he terms "non-espionage intelligence."[4] This is exactly the arena in which Quimby and his companions worked. They performed reconnaissance and carried messages; captured prisoners and cataloged troop movements.

Works that center on the role of scouts are often about whole units of partisans whose experience often blurred the lines between regular service and guerrilla fighting. For example, Lieutenant Isaac Newton Earl's scouts operated around the lower Mississippi River, partially to prevent smuggling and partially to counter Confederate guerrillas. Their actions proved crucial to the Union's successful occupation of the 600-mile stretch of the Mississippi from north of the White River in Arkansas all the way to New Orleans. A similar unit, Captain Richard Blazer's Union scouts, proved to be much less well known than their primary opponents, Mosby's Confederate Rangers.[5]

The line between scouting and spying often blurred in practice. If we think of spies as taking on secret identities, working for one side while pretending to represent the other, while scouts operated more openly as soldiers, Quimby did a bit of both. That is, he spent much of his time on the March in Confederate uniform, hoping that disguise would preserve his safety and make civilians more willing to share information. This ability to transform oneself was key to Quimby's own definition of a "good scout": "one should be quick to think, quick to act, and have a general knowledge of the geography and inhabitants of the country in which he operates, and withal he should have gentlemanly instincts. While he should be a strict partisan, he should also be possessed of a large amount of human kindness, and not be blind to the wants, acts, likes and dislikes of the enemy's home people. He should be familiar with their provincial dialect, if they have any, and have a thorough knowledge of their sympathies and hates. With all these necessary qualifications he would still be useless as a scout if he did not possess the required amount of moral courage to enable him to fly to the rescue of a friend or comrade if there be a 'greater probability of saving their life than that of losing his own.'" Quimby's own adventures would prove that he possessed all of these "necessary qualifications."

Quimby's emphasis on kindness and moral courage comes through his memoirs quite clearly. First, he makes a careful distinction between scouting and foraging. At several points he describes "bummers"—soldiers stealing food and property beyond the boundaries of organized efforts—in less than complimentary terms. Quimby and his compatriots stopped soldiers from taking food, and at one point actually returned fifteen stolen hams to a grateful planter. He seems to have been operating from a mixture of personal standards and the realization that unnecessary destruction could only hurt the Union effort by further angering civilians. Thus his memoir does not feature the scenes of unending, wanton terror and devastation that are often staples of stories about Sherman's March. Rather, Quimby explains violence and excesses away as the work of "the scalawags that were always present in armies that brought disgrace to better men."[6]

Quimby portrayed himself as having a certain sympathy for white Southerners; in part this comes across because Quimby's memoir is not ideological. He is especially conscious of class distinctions, and finds himself increasingly sympathetic to the plight of yeoman and lower-class white Southerners. He was far from alone in this sensibility; Sherman himself had drawn this line in his Special Field Orders No. 120 when he suggested that when seizing livestock, foragers should discriminate "between the rich, who are usually hostile, and the poor and industrious, usually neutral or friendly."[7] In general, Quimby paints his interactions with Southern white civilians in a positive light, flirting with young women (and ultimately courting and marrying one). In both of these ways, his memoir cuts across the more familiar narrative of tense, even angry or frightening, interactions between Sherman's soldiers and white Southerners, especially women.[8]

Quimby's many encounters with African Americans follow more familiar scripts. He clearly relied on enslaved people to guide, feed, and protect him. His missions would not have succeeded without African Americans' help and knowledge, and he realizes that, but at the same time he does not fully acknowledge them as actors in their own right. Sherman's army brought emancipation with it as it moved across the landscape, but it was hardly a march full of abolitionists. Sherman himself was not an advocate of black equality, and he did everything he could to stop newly freed people from following the army along its route. Quimby's encounters with African Americans run the gamut. At times he is deeply appreciative and grateful for their help; at times he treats them with a kind of casual cruelty that was also, unfortunately, typical for the times.[9]

When Quimby wrote his memoir at the turn of the twentieth century, veterans from both sides were engaged in a prodigious effort to describe, preserve, catalog, and make sense of their wartime experiences. They organized themselves into powerful groups such as the Grand Army of the Republic, the Society of the Army of the Tennessee, the Military Order of the Loyal Legion of the United States in the North, and the United Confederate Veterans in the South. Veterans held reunions—sometimes of one or two regiments, sometimes of whole organizations, and sometimes joint Blue-Gray Reunions. They wrote for publications such as *The Century* or *Confederate Veteran*, and for newspapers all over the country. We don't know whether Quimby was a member of a veterans organization or attended reunions. We do know that he wrote, and that he maintained active connections and correspondence with many of his fellow veterans.[10] Quimby appears to have been untroubled by his wartime service—at least emotionally. The physical toll was greater, and its effects shaped his later life. But his memoir is written as a lark and an adventure, and if he struggled with demons, he kept them to himself.[11]

George W. Quimby was born on August 10, 1842, in Newark (Licking County), Ohio. His family had emigrated from Ireland to the American colonies in the early eighteenth century, and his grandfather, Benjamin, had been born in Vermont in the early 1770s. Benjamin Quimby attended Yale College and married Jane Lain in 1800. They had eight children, including George Quimby's father, Omar A. Quimby, born in 1808 in Lunenberg, Vermont. In early 1834, Omar married Amanda Crippen, a fellow Vermonter, in St. Albans, and sometime shortly thereafter the family moved to Ohio. Omar was a farmer and a blacksmith. George was the third of seven children, all but the eldest born in Ohio.[12] Omar and his family moved to Wisconsin in 1850, where they lived first in Berlin and then in New London. Finally, in 1857, Omar purchased a plot of land in Waupaca, Wisconsin, and settled down. He helped to organize the new township of DuPont, and also served over the years as town treasurer and postmaster.[13]

Little is known about George's early life. When the Civil War broke out, he was living in Wisconsin. Four days after he turned twenty, Quimby and his older brother David enlisted in Company B, 32nd Wisconsin Infantry, in Ripon, Wisconsin.[14] George was six feet tall, with light hair and blue eyes, and he gave his occupation as "farmer." Six weeks later, he was in Oshkosh, where he was officially mustered in as a sergeant in Company B for three years.[15] It took another few weeks before the 32nd Wisconsin finally left the state and headed south.

Quimby and his comrades arrived in Memphis on November 3, 1862, and were assigned to the fifth brigade, second division of the right wing of the XIII Corps, Department of the Tennessee, under General William T. Sherman and ultimately General Ulysses S. Grant. They were quartered south of the city near Fort Pickering, although not for long. The 32nd played little direct role in the multiple attempts to take Vicksburg that occupied the army during the winter and early spring of 1862–1863. Rather, they spent December 1862 moving around Northern Mississippi, sometimes guarding bridges and trestles. In January they spent a few weeks at Jackson, only to be ordered back to Memphis in early February, where they remained on provost duty until November 1863.[16]

We don't know what Quimby thought of his first year of service, although given the zeal with which he recalled his later adventures, we might imagine he found his time there a little dull. He seems to have gotten into some kind of trouble, for on May 30, 1863, he was reduced in rank to private by the 32nd's Colonel James H. Howe. But all of that would change in late November 1863, when the 32nd Wisconsin left Memphis to take on Confederate General Nathan Bedford Forrest's notorious cavalry in western Tennessee.[17]

In late December, Quimby and his fellow soldiers skirmished with the Confederates around Lafayette, Tennessee. The weather was wet, the marching hard, and because of a pair of ill-fitting boots, Quimby found himself lagging behind the rest of the regiment, accompanied by his bunkmate, John A. White. As they hustled to catch up, they found themselves approaching a group of men, and "one can imagine our surprise when we found 120 rebel carbines leveled on us, accompanied by a demand to surrender. There was nothing left for us but to comply with their polite request."[18] Quimby and White promised to stick together, and to try to escape at the earliest opportunity. Along with another nine Union prisoners, they were marched south at a rapid place. When horses were available, they were allowed to ride at the rear of the columns, and Quimby was struck by Forrest's habit of moving his men in small groups and along multiple roads. Initially they camped in "negro huts"—slave cabins—and suffered from exposure to the cold and elements. That being said, however, Quimby seemed to bear his captors no great ill will, noting that "we fared as well as did our guards, they dividing equally with us such food as they obtained. No harsh or abusive language was used toward us."[19]

On New Year's Day 1864, Quimby, White, and their fellow prisoners settled in on a plantation about fifty miles south of Memphis. The officers moved into the main house, while the guards and prisoners crowded into an overseer's cabin. It was so cold that "to escape would have been suicidal," although Quimby continued to keep his eyes open for an opportunity. At last he and White took advantage of lax supervision and they slipped away, heading west toward the Mississippi River. Quimby suffered from sharp knee pains, and an African American hid them for the night in his unginned cotton.[20]

They were less fortunate in their choice of hiding spot the following day. Upon knocking at the door of a plantation kitchen, Quimby and White found themselves greeted by a shotgun-wielding white woman, who promptly brought them to her Confederate officer husband. Initially, to the Yankees' surprise, the Southerner lavished hospitality on them, claiming that "his sense of honor would not permit him to interfere with the comfort or pleasure of his guests; that we were now his guests, and he must be governed accordingly." He let them go on their way, even giving them directions to the town of Austin on the Mississippi River, where Quimby and White could find Union gunboats and safety.[21]

Quimby's bum knee notwithstanding, they made it to the town, all the way to the banks of the Mississippi. As they tried to hail a Union ship, they ran into a group of Confederate smugglers, who plied Quimby and White with food and drinks (which they declined). At last the drunken smugglers wrote out paroles for White and Quimby, which they signed (even as they indicated that the Union Army would never accept them as valid), and brought them aboard their steamship, loaded with contraband and headed for Memphis. After two or three more days, they finally arrived in Memphis. The boat was seized, the smugglers put on trial, and on January 13, 1864, Quimby returned to service with the rest of his regiment.[22]

After six weeks of excitement, captures, and escapes, Quimby might have welcomed a stretch of provost duty in Memphis, but it was not to be. In late January, they left Memphis again, this time for Vicksburg, where they joined the XVI Corps and took part in Sherman's Meridian campaign, destroying railroads and bridges across Mississippi and Alabama. On June 28, in Courtland, Alabama, the 32nd Wisconsin snuck down the banks of the Tennessee River and surrounded a group of over 400 Confederate soldiers, killed and wounded 17, took another 49 prisoners, and captured wagons, horses, and other equipment. From there they marched to Decatur, Alabama, for picket duty. One of Quimby's comrades fondly recalled trading with the women of Decatur, offering them snuff in exchange for fresh vegetables and butter, "great users of snuff they were in this locality."[23] On July 24, the regiment was guarding a wagon train a few miles outside of town when they were attacked by Confederate cavalry. Although the wagon train was saved, several Union soldiers were captured. They continued skirmishing the following day, losing half a dozen men in the process.[24]

At this point, the 32nd Wisconsin moved again, this time to play a more active role in Sherman's army. They took part in the final siege of Atlanta, fighting at Jonesboro, Georgia, on July 29–30 and then the last battle for Atlanta. They pursued Hood's retreating army, and then moved into Atlanta proper in early October. As Sherman's army made ready for their March, the 32nd Wisconsin was transferred to the XVII Corps, under General Frank P. Blair.[25] Here George Quimby's story parted company from that of his fellow troops. While Quimby became a scout, the 32nd Wisconsin's men marched along with the Right Wing of Sherman's army.

Sherman's March, both from Atlanta to Savannah during November and December 1864, and then from Savannah up through the Carolinas between February and April 1865, was one of the most significant Union campaigns of the Civil War. Its mythic aspects, stories of swaths of destruction fifty miles wide, of stolen silver, and burning homes, have often overshadowed its more complex realities and real strategic significance. In the fall of 1864, Robert E. Lee's Army of Northern Virginia and Ulysses S. Grant's Army of the Potomac were stuck in trenches outside of Petersburg, Virginia. They would remain there for nine months. Sherman breaking through and taking Atlanta on September 2 ensured that Abraham Lincoln would be reelected in November. Soon after he occupied Atlanta, Sherman decided to evacuate the city's civilian population—he wanted the city to be a purely military base, didn't want to deal with feeding or protecting civilians, or guarding his men against guerrillas and spies. He also didn't want to have to detail soldiers to hold the city as in Memphis or New Orleans. Accused of being unduly harsh and punitive by both the mayor of Atlanta and John Bell Hood, Sherman replied simply that "war is cruelty and you can not refine it."[26]

His next plan was to march across Georgia, 285 miles to Savannah, making it "howl," living off the land, and destroying everything that could aid the Confederacy. This was risky, because he would be cut off from his base, and John Bell Hood still had 40,000 men in northern Alabama. Sherman finally convinced Grant and Lincoln to allow him to undertake this major movement, and in mid-November, the men began to prepare.[27] Those soldiers who were too unwell to make the trip to Savannah were sent to the rear, along with excess baggage. Trains were loaded with supplies and sent away. And then commenced, in Sherman's laconic phrase, "the special work of destruction." Under the direction of Colonel Orlando Poe, the men pried up railroads and melted and twisted the ties, essentially erasing the Western and Atlantic Rail Line. Within the city limits, they turned to buildings, specifically the remnants of Confederate infrastructure: factories, railroad stations, storehouses, and the roundhouse. First the men used battering rams, heeding Poe's orders that they not use fire (too dangerous). But by November 11, soldiers began to burn houses throughout the town. While Union troops were detailed to guard some buildings—churches in particular—fires, authorized and not, were set each night. On November 14, Poe ordered that everything not destroyed be set ablaze. The fires continued through the night of November 15–16.

Sherman's army of 62,000 men did not march across Georgia in a single swath, mowing down everything in their path. Rather, it was subdivided into two wings, each one consisting of two corps: the XV and XVII in the Right Wing (with the 32nd Wisconsin), the XIV and XX in the Left Wing. General Oliver O. Howard commanded the Right Wing, with Peter J. Osterhaus leading the XV Corps and Francis Preston Blair Jr. the XVII Corps. General Henry W. Slocum took charge of the Left Wing, with Jefferson C. Davis (no relation to the Confederate president) leading the XIV Corps and Alpheus S. Williams the XX Corps. Sherman initially rode with the Left Wing. Almost 5,000 cavalrymen under Judson Kilpatrick wove back and forth. What this meant was that the March progressed in a total of four columns, each separated from the next by a number of miles.

Although Savannah was Sherman's ultimate destination, he used the wings to obscure his intentions, having the Right Wing feint toward Macon and the Left toward Augusta. The columns moved at a leisurely pace, about ten or fifteen miles a day. They didn't face much organized opposition, although as Quimby's story shows, Confederate cavalry under General Joseph Wheeler was a constant threat.

Before setting out, Sherman tried to set some ground rules. His Special Field Orders No. 120 ordered his men to "forage liberally on the country," and "to destroy mills, houses, cotton-gins, etc.," but within limits. The foraging parties were supposed to be regularized and under the control of "discreet" officers; soldiers were not supposed to enter homes; should the army be left "unmolested," Southern property was also supposed to be left alone. Significantly, Sherman also ordered that when seizing livestock, his men ought to discriminate "between the rich, who are usually hostile, and the poor and industrious, usually neutral or friendly." As for African Americans, Sherman was willing to permit commanders to put "able-bodied" men who could "be of service" into pioneer corps, but urged them to be mindful of their limited supplies. Well aware of his logistical limitations, Sherman wanted his officers to leave the newly freed women and children behind.[28]

These rules were often ignored. Union soldiers terrorized Southerners— both white and black. They stole from them and destroyed what they could not carry off. Sherman's men took on the moniker "bummer," originally an epithet meaning a skulker or a thief, and used it as a badge of pride. At the same time, in other situations Union soldiers and African Americans might work together, or share small kindnesses. Sherman's soldiers were not, by and large, motivated by a deep-seated belief in black equality. But whether they liked it or not, they functioned as an army of emancipation and liberation, freeing enslaved people with every mile they marched.[29]

The soldiers of the Right Wing (including the 32nd Wisconsin) moved out of Atlanta, and marched back through Jonesboro and McDonough. They moved through Butts, Monroe, Jasper, and Jones counties, burning textile factories and barns, taking horses, and leaving dead ones in their wake. Much of their mission centered on destroying the railroads, tearing up the rails, and twisting them into loops and corkscrews that came to be called "Sherman's neckties." The March featured few actual battles, but one took place outside the small town of Griswoldville, where a small group of Georgians attacked a Union brigade at the rear of the XV Corps. When the smoke cleared, the Union men were aghast to realize, that "old grey-haired and weakly-looking men and little boys, not over 15 years old, lay dead or writhing in pain. I did pity those boys, they almost all who could talk said the Rebel cavalry gathered them up and forced them in."[30] This did not slow the pace of the March, however. The Right Wing continued moving, crossing the Oconee River on pontoon bridges, and sweeping through the small towns of sandy-soiled eastern Georgia. They raided Swainsboro and Statesboro, and finally approached Savannah in early December.

The soldiers of the Left Wing, Sherman riding along with them, traveled in much the same fashion. Their first major destination was Milledgeville, Georgia's capital at the time. Georgia's governor and state legislators fled in advance of the Union Army; Sherman and his men marched into town on November 22–23. The men plundered the state house, threw books out the windows of the state library, blew up the arsenal, and burned the railroad depot. Only a few private homes were burned, generally those belonging to prominent Confederates.[31] A few days later, as they continued toward the coast, Sherman joined up with the Right Wing. The Left Wing soldiers arrived at Camp Lawton outside Millen, a Confederate prison built to relieve overcrowding at Andersonville. Open for only six weeks, the prison had been hastily evacuated. All Sherman's men found were graves.[32] By December 10 the two wings met up.

Savannah was still home to about 10,000 Confederate troops, so Sherman's men bypassed the city, focusing their efforts instead on Fort McAllister, where the Ogeechee River emptied into Ossabaw Sound.[33] This was the occasion for one of Quimby's great adventures. They captured the Fort on December 13, allowing a supply line to be opened for the first time in a month, meaning that the men could also receive mail for the first time since Atlanta. Sherman decided to try to wait out the Confederates in Savannah, but after a few days, on December 17, he wrote to General Hardee demanding a surrender. After enduring a few days of bombardment, Hardee and his men slipped out of the city (Sherman had left them an escape route). On December 22, the day after riding triumphantly into the city, Sherman sent Lincoln his famous telegram:

His Excellency
Prest. Lincoln

I beg to present to you as a Christmas gift the City of Savannah
with 150 heavy guns & plenty of ammunition & also about 25,000
bales of Cotton.

W. T. Sherman
Major General[34]

Sherman and his men spent about a month in and around Savannah, using
this as an opportunity to rest up and resupply. The men of the 32nd Wisconsin spent the New Year in and around Savannah, and then moved (along
with the rest of the XVII Corps) to Beaufort, South Carolina, and from
there to Pocotaligo.[35]

They then embarked on the second phase of their great campaign, the
March through the Carolinas. Though less well known than the March to
the Sea, it was—particularly in South Carolina—even more destructive.
There the Union veterans vented their anger on the place they believed began
the Civil War. Sherman himself recalled, somewhat disingenuously: "Somehow our men had got the idea that South Carolina was the cause of all our
troubles; her people were the first to fire on Fort Sumter, had been in a great
hurry to precipitate the country into civil war; and therefore on them should
fall the scourge of war in its worst form. . . . I saw and felt that we would not
be able longer to restrain our men as we had done in Georgia . . . and I would
not restrain the army lest its vigor and energy should be impaired."[36] Too, the
first days and weeks after Savannah (or in Quimby's case, Pocotaligo) also
held the toughest terrain of the March: the Salkahatchie swamps.

On February 2 and 3, the 32nd Wisconsin, along with the rest of the
Right Wing, fought the battle of Rivers Bridge, described by Alanson
Wood as "the hardest contested battle our regiment was ever engaged in."
The Union men fought Confederates under General Lafayette McLaws over
a crossing point on the Salkahatchie River. Wood recalled that the battle
was fought "in water from a knee to a waist deep all day, and a hand to hand
contest driving the enemy back by charging on them time after time, only
gaining a rod or two at each rally made."[37] Although South Carolinians
have long hailed Rivers Bridge as a "last stand" against Sherman, it only
slowed but did not stop the March's constant forward progress.

The men moved through South Carolina, burning churches and private homes, tearing up mile after mile of railroad tracks, venting their anger on the cradle of secession. Their goal was Columbia, the state capital, and they reached the outskirts on February 15. On the night of February 16, Columbia burned—the result of fires set by both retreating Confederates and Union soldiers. Chaos and looting ruled the night, fueled by burning cotton and barrels of liquor.[38] But the March kept moving.

The marchers stopped briefly in Cheraw, South Carolina, on March 2, and then crossed the Pee Dee River into North Carolina. Sherman wanted his men to rein themselves in after the excesses of South Carolina, in a nod to the Unionists in North Carolina, but this did not entirely happen. The troops marched toward Fayetteville, and from there the Right Wing headed to Goldsboro while the Left feinted toward Raleigh. While the March featured few outright battles (with Griswoldville and Rivers Bridge as exceptions), Sherman was now being more directly opposed by his old opponent, Confederate General Joseph Johnston, and his army. The two sides fought at both Averasboro and Bentonville in March.[39]

After a long rest in Goldsboro, during which Sherman actually traveled to Virginia to meet with Grant and Lincoln, the March resumed in early April. On the thirteenth, they took Raleigh, their third state capital. On April 17, Sherman and Johnston met at a small farmhouse near Durham, North Carolina, known as the Bennett Place, to hash out surrender terms. Sherman's were initially quite generous, offering a general amnesty. But in the charged climate following Lincoln's assassination, the terms were rejected. Ultimately, on April 26, Johnston's Confederates surrendered under terms like those at Appomattox. The Great March was over.[40]

Well, almost over. Sherman's troops continued to march north, through Virginia to Washington, DC. There, on March 24, they took part in the Grand Review of the Union Armies, marching for hours down Pennsylvania Avenue.[41] From there, the 32nd Wisconsin went into camp at Crystal Springs, near Washington. They were officially mustered out on June 12, 1865, and headed home to Wisconsin.[42]

George Quimby did not go with them. As he indicated in his memoir, he was offered a commission in a new regiment, the 128th United States Colored Troops. He was officially mustered in as a second lieutenant in Hilton Head, South Carolina, on June 20, 1865, six days after he was officially discharged from the 32nd Wisconsin. While stationed in Beaufort, Quimby renewed his acquaintance with Miss Mary E. Stevenson, and the two were married on August 1, 1865. His service in the USCT appeared unremarkable for the next year, until he was "tried by a General Court Martial upon the following charges: Contempt and disrespectful conduct toward his commanding officer," and "conduct unbecoming an officer and a gentleman." Quimby was found guilty and discharged dating from July 20, 1866.[43]

What little we know about George Quimby's life after his military service comes from an entry in a local history, and his various Civil War pension applications. He seemed to have inherited his father and grandfather's wandering tendencies, moving west several times during the nineteenth century. He and Mary had a total of eleven children between 1866 and 1888, five sons and six daughters. In 1880, the Quimbys (who had six living children at the time) were living in Arkansas and had already lived in Wisconsin, Nebraska, and South Dakota; George was working as a real estate agent at the time, although he had earlier tried his hand at farming.[44]

Sixteen years later, Quimby and his family were living in Verdigre, Nebraska (Knox County). In fact, he had helped found the town, buying property and then platting out the lots in 1887. He devoted considerable effort to making sure that the town would be served by the railroad. He also briefly ran a newspaper and served as a justice of the peace in Nebraska.[45] In 1896, Quimby was fifty-three, his health had declined considerably, and he was described as "wholly unable to earn a support by manual labor," due to a laundry list of ailments including sciatic rheumatism, piles, quinsy, catarrh, and severe bronchitis, as well as still suffering the aftereffects of his long-ago gunshot wound.

In 1898, Quimby moved to Bellingham, Washington, his last major move. Despite his many ailments, he lived for another twenty-eight years. It's likely that he wrote his memoirs during this period of retirement. His story of being captured by General Forrest's men was published in the *National Tribune* in 1903.[46] Mary died in 1918. By the time of his death on October 21, 1926, in Everson, Washington, he was an invalid, living with his son Fred and in need of constant care. He suffered from cataracts and could barely move without aid.[47] One can only imagine how diminishing this must have been for one so active and adventurous in his earlier years.

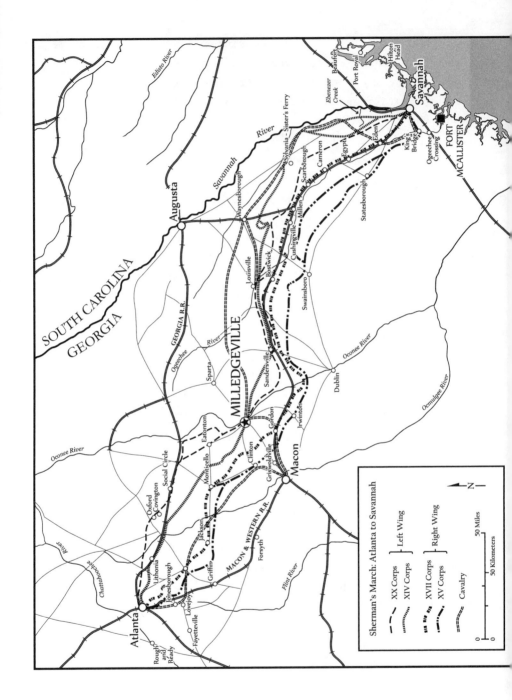

Sherman's March: Atlanta to Savannah

Left Wing
    XX Corps
    XIV Corps

Right Wing
    XVII Corps
    XV Corps

Cavalry

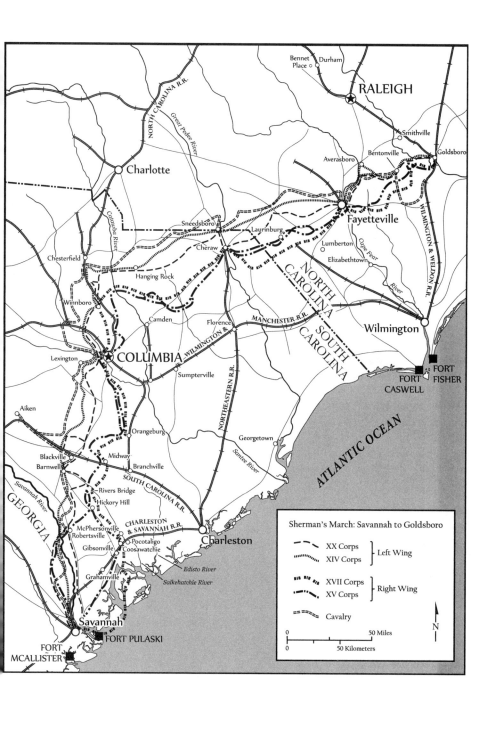

Bennet Place ○
Durham

RALEIGH

Smithville

NORTH CAROLINA R.R.

Charlotte

Great Pedee River

Averasboro
Bentonville

Goldsboro

Sneedsboro
Laurinburg

Fayetteville

WILMINGTON & WELDON R.R.

Cheraw
Lumberton

Cape Fear River

Chesterfield

Elizabethtown

Catawba River

Hanging Rock

NORTH CAROLINA

Winnboro

Camden
Florence

MANCHESTER R.R.

SOUTH CAROLINA

Columbia

Wilmington

Lexington

WILMINGTON &

COLUMBIA

Sumpterville

NORTHEASTERN R.R.

FORT
CASWELL

FORT
FISHER

Aiken

Orangeburg

Georgetown

Santee River

ATLANTIC OCEAN

Blackville
Barnwell

Midway
Branchville

SOUTH CAROLINA R.R.

Savannah River

Rivers Bridge
Hickory Hill

GEORGIA

CHARLESTON
& SAVANNAH R.R.

McPhersonville
Robertsville
Gibsonville

Pocotaligo
Coosawatchie

Charleston

Edisto River

Grahamville

Salkehatchie River

Savannah

FORT PULASKI

FORT
MCALLISTER

Sherman's March: Savannah to Goldsboro

- - - XX Corps ⎤
········· XIV Corps ⎦ Left Wing

▪▮▪ ▮▪▮ XVII Corps ⎤
-·-·- XV Corps ⎦ Right Wing

═ ═ ═ Cavalry

0   50 Miles

0   50 Kilometers

N

The Great March
To the Sea

and

The Campaign Of
The Carolinas

========

By a Scout

========

Part

Vol. I

THE
PERFECT SCOUT

George W. Quimby's Introduction

IT MIGHT BE SAID that the subject matter of the following reminiscences has been so many times more ably written, that it is now becoming threadbare, so to speak. The writer can only offer the excuse of the French priest, who, while deploring war, said: "I was not a priest until after the great wars; God pardon me, but I like still to tell tales of Jena and Austerlitz and of what we did in those days of victory. To kill men! The idea now fills me with horror, and yet I like nothing better than to talk of those days of battle."

Again, having been present with three thousand others, listening to a lecture by a prominent retired general on "The March to the Sea," I overheard a lady say to another: "One would think, from that lecture, that Sherman had an army of generals and no privates."

PART I

The Great March to the Sea

I

Introduction to Scouting

Alas, in Greece how ill things ordered are.
When trophies rise for victories in war
Men count the praise not theirs who did the deed,
But give alone to him who led the meed.
—Euripides

FROM TIME IMMEMORIAL it has been the custom of all army commanders, both civilized, semi-civilized, and barbarians, in time of war, to have a small band or corps of carefully selected men to operate on the flanks or rear of their respective armies for the purpose of watching the enemy and to report any change of position or suspicious movements.

These scouts have never been considered as spies, and never performed duties as such, and were always entitled to the treatment of any other branch of the army should they be so unfortunate as to be taken prisoners by the enemy.[1]

This rule prevailed in both the Federal and Confederate Armies during the late war. Generals Grant, Sherman, Thomas, and in fact all other independent commanders, always kept a corps of scouts numbering from two to fifty men, whose duties were oftentimes most arduous when the balance of the armies were having their easiest time because, when an army is lying in camp in great apparent security, it is doubly necessary for the commanding officer to keep himself posted as to the whereabouts and all the movements of his opponents. The commanding officers have always been looked upon as the brains, the soldiers the brawn, and the scouts the eyes of the army.

As an illustration of this necessity, I will state that during the armistice between Generals Sherman and Hood at Atlanta,[2] which lasted several days, General Howard's scouts reported daily to General Sherman what was being done by Hood's army.

The rules of war governing an armistice are such that neither party of the armistice is permitted to move their army or any part of it with a view to bettering their position, either for the present or future operations. Notwithstanding these rules, General Hood did move his army, and at the hour the armistice closed, his army was crossing the Chattahoochie River, twenty miles away.[3]

This movement the scouts were able to report daily to General Sherman. I wish to state here that General Sherman apparently paid no attention to these reports, leaving the impression on our minds that he thought we were misrepresenting it. However, on the last day of grace we rushed up to his tent and reported that we had "seen them crossing the river in force." He smiled and turned to the Adjutant General (Colonel Dalt)[4] and said: "Well, General, I think that we had better be moving. Have the bugle sounded, I think we have him where we want him." Then it was that we discovered that he had heeded our reports and had the tents all struck, wagons packed, and the men in ranks, so that in five minutes the whole army was moving.

In describing the qualifications necessary of a good scout, I can only say that one should be quick to think, quick to act, and have a general knowledge of the geography and inhabitants of the country in which he operates, and withal he should have gentlemanly instincts. While he should be a strict partisan, he should also be possessed of a large amount of human kindness, and not be blind to the wants, acts, likes, and dislikes of the enemy's home people. He should be familiar with their provincial dialect, if they have any, and have a thorough knowledge of their sympathies and hates.

With all these necessary qualifications he would still be useless as a scout if he did not possess the required amount of moral courage to enable him to fly to the rescue of a friend or comrade if there be a "greater probability of saving their life than that of losing his own."

It is a well-established fact that the Indians of the Western plains have had greater fear of a dozen plainsmen or "cowboys" than of a hundred soldiers. This is accounted for by the fact that the cowboys move and act as individuals, and none but "good men and true" are tolerated in their midst, while the soldiers move as a machine, thus enabling the Indians to do their "deviltry" and escape to distant settlements to repeat their outrages.

This is why a small party of guerrillas, or partisan rangers, are more annoying to an invading army than ten times their number when organized in a more compact body.[5] It will be remembered that General Sherman had no corps of scouts immediately at his headquarters, but General Howard, commanding the right wing of the army, had organized one under the immediate command of Captain William Duncan of Company K, 15th Illinois Cavalry, which always had their camp with his headquarters. General Slocum, commanding the left wing, also had a corps of scouts who remained with him. General Kilpatrick, commanding the cavalry, had also a corps of scouts under Lieutenant Griffin. Sometimes General Sherman would be with one wing of the army and again with the other. At whichever he happened to be, he made use of the scouts nearest at hand, giving his order, if convenient, through that wing commander, so that where history speaks of "Sherman's Scouts," it may refer to those of the right wing or of the left, as the case may be.[6]

The corps under Captain Duncan, which started on the trip to the sea, consisted of Sergeant M. J. Amick, Jerry Phelan, and Robert Collins of Company K, 15th Illinois Cavalry Regiment; Pat Wallace and Ed Daugherty of, I think, an Indiana Regiment;[7] Sergeant George W. Quimby [the author] of the 32nd Wisconsin Infantry; George Matchett of an Illinois Regiment whose home was near Momence, Illinois;[8] Joe Bedoll, I think from the 43rd Indiana;[9] Jim Taylor and Bill Smith, whose Regiment I have forgotten;[10] Job Dawson and Barney Burns, the witty and poetical Irishmen, who, if I remember correctly, were from the 100th Indiana;[11] and last but not least in importance, _____ Gillet, an old-time scout since the beginning of the war, a man of good sense and judgment, with much dignity and a large experience. He was a man of few words, never boasting of his past glorious services. He had been a scout under Buell, Thomas, and McP[h]erson and was regarded by us as an oracle on all questions pertaining to the proper maneuvering of scouts.

Each of these scouts received from the secret service fund, in addition to their regular pay, $150.00 per month. They were selected on the recommendation of their Regimental and Brigade Commanders and were to serve during good behavior. They were expected to, and did, provide their own arms and horses, but were furnished with ammunition, forage, and rations.

We were allowed a good four-mule wagon to carry our baggage and camp outfit. This was under charge of a corporal, who was wagon master, quartermaster, and generalissimo who had charge of all our camp and marching paraphernalia, and dour servants when we were absent on a scout. Each of us had a special contraband[12] servant whose duty it was to care for our horses and to lead our extra horse in the column when on the march. In addition there was a teamster, cooks, etc. All these were refugees and were under the control of the corporal, who saw to it that they performed their duty promptly and well.

We generally used a fresh horse each day, starting usually at three o'clock in the morning so as to get beyond the foragers before they had got far advanced.[13] We scarcely ever returned to the same camp at night, because the columns were nearly every day on the march, so we would be notified each morning as to the probable camping place the following night, which would be from twelve to twenty miles from the preceding. We scarcely ever went directly to the front of the column, leaving that for the advance guard, but went oblique of the army to the right or left, and sometimes away to the rear, as required by the general commanding. Again, we sometimes took dispatches from one column to another, when the distance was great and the intervening territory was unoccupied by our troops. Also on some occasions we were sent on long journeys to destroy some railroad or telegraph. Frequently we went to a distance of thirty or forty miles from any of our columns, weaving our way through the scattered bands of troops and home guard, as they were called, and furloughed Confederate soldiers. We had very little opposition until after the Oconee River was crossed,[14] when we began to encounter General Wheeler's cavalry,[15] which had gained our front, passing round our flank from the Tennessee raid. Our force would be sometimes divided and sent in different directions on separate errands. Occasionally one or two of the scouts would remain and ride with the column for a day to rest up. At the end of this campaign, we estimated that we had averaged seventy miles per day for the entire trip. It is unnecessary to say that many horses were used up. Horses, however, were cheap with us. They were, of course, taken from the planters; we, usually leaving the jaded ones in their stead. It was our custom for each to keep one or two good ones in reserve in the care of our servants to be used only on special occasions when an unusually hard trip was to be made.

We had made it a rule among ourselves never to do any foraging (except in the matter of horses, and Wheeler's men did that also), and never to ask for anything without offering pay for the same. We had a double reason for this rule. First, we were liable to be captured at any time, and if, after

foraging we should be captured near the scene of our so-called depredations, it would be very apt to go hard with us.

Put yourself in their place, and then judge.

Secondly, perhaps no other branch of the service enabled one to see
the inside of secession and to become fairly well acquainted with the true
feelings and general kindness of the individuals of the South, especially of
the families and the old men and returned wounded soldiers. We gradually
learned to respect, and then to sympathize with, them and finally would as
soon thought of robbing our mother as those kind people of Georgia.

Some of our boys had come into possession of $35,000 of Confederate
money, mostly in $20 and $100 bills and this being distributed among the
whole, we were able to liquidate all our obligations without straining our
purse very much.

It is but just to say, however, that only in the case of very poor people
would they consent to receive any remuneration. We soon became accustomed to their methods of receiving strangers and never, within my recollection, did anyone decline to furnish a dinner of feed for our horses,
if within their power to supply them. It is true that we were dressed in
Confederate uniforms, and often considered as Confederate soldiers; but in
many instances after being informed that we were "Yankees," it seemed to
make little or no difference in their conduct toward us.

As a rule we found them badly informed as to the true state of affairs—
they nearly always claiming that their armies had always been successful in
battle. The young ladies especially, feeling the most free to combat our success, nearly always ended the discussion by adding with a very pleasant twin-
kle of the eye, "Just wait till we get you where we want you." These discus-
sions never appeared to make any difference as to our standing as guests and
we were nearly always invited to call on them again when the war was over.

In order that the reader may understand our method of procedure, I will
state that we usually marched in a body with two men from one hundred
to two hundred yards in advance and the same number of men the same
distance in the rear of the main body, keeping a sharp lookout for traps
and surprises, for when we got below the Oconee, we found the soldiers
in Wheeler's "Critter Company" about as sharp and skillful in laying traps
and ambushes as we were. It is probably safe to say that we exchanged shots
with large or small parties of "Rebs" on an average of once every day of
the entire campaign. Many of these scraps were without result for either

side, but on the whole we were decidedly ahead of the game, for while we lost but four of our thirteen scouts, we turned over to the Provost marshal fifty-two prisoners at various times. This does not include a large number of men taken by us whom we regarded as "irresponsible," men of no benefit to us or the enemy. Nor does it include the number captured by us and whom we were unable to bring to camp before they were retaken by their friends or escaped from us. This last number was by no means small as this narrative will show hereafter.

We had private signals among ourselves that could be used when in sight of the enemy without being detected. In this way, suppose the advance should suddenly come in view of a small party of Rebs and it was thought safe and advisable to try to capture them, a signal would be made to those in the rear to "lay a trap," or "move up lively," or "wait till we parley," and so on. Suppose the trap decided on, the advance would fire a shot or two and then run back on the road expecting to be followed by the Rebs. The main body would drop out to the right and left, and the advance would pass through the trap and go on to the two rear guards, by which time the pursuers would have passed the "trap." Then all hands closed in on the gentlemen and the game would be ended. This scheme did not always work for they soon got to be wary as a fox. The reader must keep in mind the fact that the entire South is, or was, entirely covered with a forest of open oak or pine woods, and where no special mention is made of a clear field, it must be understood that the event took place in the open woods.

When a capture was made, the prisoners would be disarmed, after which (if considered safe), some of the captors would produce a canteen and all hands would "smile."

I want to say right here that we captured many of Wheeler's men, and several of ours, who never reached a permanent prison but succeeded in making their escape before the main column was reached, were captured by them.

A friendly feeling came to exist between them, not but that each did their whole duty, but remember that we were oftentimes many miles from our command and had about all we could do to arrive there ourselves, much less to bring a lot of prisoners along. We could not kill them, because we did not particularly desire to be killed by them should at any time the tables be turned, which sometimes happened.[16]

2

Fayetteville

Borne down at length on every side,
Compelled to flight, they scatter wide.

ON THE MORNING of November 15, 1864, our band of scouts, numbering thirteen, were instructed by General Howard to join those of General Kilpatrick, numbering about thirty, under Chief of Scouts Griffin,[1] to proceed on the Fayetteville road to the right of Jonesboro.[2] As near as I can remember, we had proceeded about thirty miles when we encountered the enemy's pickets, who fired an alarm and retreated in haste, rapidly followed by the scouts. Chief Griffin set the pace, flying like the wind, in an endeavor to overtake the pickets and surprise the main force, which was known to be in camp about two miles distant. The force consisted of a regiment of cavalry, who were nicely fixed up in comfortable quarters near the roadside. It must be remembered that Griffin's scouts were armed with a carbine and two or more navy revolvers with ammunition galore, while Howard's scouts dispensed with the carbine but added another revolver. It was not uncommon to see one with a revolver on each hip, one in each boot leg, and perhaps another hanging over the pommel of his saddle. Carbines and sabers were regarded by us as useless and cumbrous ornaments; all our fighting being done on the wing, so to speak. We, as scouts, were not supposed to engage in exchanging shots with the enemy except when unavoidable, and many a mild reproof we received from General Howard for unnecessarily having little "spats" with General Wheeler's scouts or other patrols.

Our Chief of Scouts, Captain Duncan, of course, outranked Lieutenant Griffin, and under ordinary military rules should have taken command of the entire force of scouts. However, in this particular kind of service, little attention was paid to rank when away from camp. In fact, I have many times seen scouts remonstrating with their chiefs on questions of immediate interest to themselves and party.

I use the word "remonstrate" for want of a more proper one. What I mean is, in a case where we would discover a small party of Rebs without knowing their real number or position, whether it is advisable to charge them with a view to capturing them.

On this occasion Lieutenant Griffin took the lead, followed by the entire party as fast as their horses could run, firing and yelling like devils incarnate. The varying speed of the different horses caused them to scatter somewhat along the road, thereby extending the column to perhaps half a mile. Those in the rear kept up the yelling and firing just the same as those in front, thus undoubtedly causing the "Johns" to think that a million Yanks were coming. At any rate, when I, having a very slow horse, arrived at the camp, I found it abandoned with the scouts in pursuit of the enemy. The tents and shacks still stood, fires were still burning, and the kettles over the fires evidently cooking their dinner.

I had discovered in the race that my pistols, having been exposed to a drenching rain and I having neglected to clean and recharge them, would not go off.

I came to a halt off the camp and immediately two "Johns" came into camp near me and were evidently very much surprised to find it abandoned. They had been out foraging and getting a lot of bread baked. One had a musket slung over his back by its gun-sling, the other had only a revolver in his belt. It is difficult to tell who was most surprised, they or I, and for a moment it was uncertain which would demand the other to surrender. I was largely influenced by the fact that my pistols could not be fired, but a sudden inspiration occurred to me and I presented my harmless weapons and ordered them to surrender, which they very cheerfully did. I ordered them to throw their weapons to the ground and ride a few steps away and dismount. By this capture I secured a beautiful bay mare that held her own in speed with any steed in the force. The revolver, too, was a good one and in good condition. I also secured a very much better saddle and bridle than the one I had heretofore used. I felt very proud of my capture, especially of the mare, because a scout is not "in it" if he is not well mounted.

This camp was situated near Fayetteville, several miles southwest of Jonesboro. I bent the musket barrel around a tree and transferred my effects to the back of my beautiful mare and was deliberating as to what to do with my prisoners when a regiment of cavalry, the advance of one of Kilpatrick's columns, made its appearance on a road that intersected the one near where I stood. The colonel came to a halt at the junction of the roads and wanted to know the cause of all this shouting and shooting he had heard and hastened to, which I explained to him.

While we were standing thus, General Kilpatrick and staff came toward us from the direction from which the colonel had come. The colonel saluted the general and said: "General, here are two prisoners which this man," pointing to me, "has just brought in." Old "Kil" then broke loose, and if any soldier can remember how he used to recite his Sunday School lesson backwards, he will know what took place. It was something like this, but came so near taking my breath that I cannot be positive as to the exact words. "Colonel, blank blank your blank soul, if you take another prisoner on this trip I'll cut your blank blank head off; we did not come out on this trip to fight these blank blank of blank; don't stop to fight them but run over them." Now, I am positive that these are nearly the words used. It made a deep impression on me at the time, and I thought he must certainly be a little off in his head. However, when I talked the matter over afterwards with one of his scouts, he said it was only for effect, that prisoners frequently escape and he wanted the word conveyed to the Rebs that he had come down there on "business" this time.

It was apparent this was as far in this direction as the cavalry intended to go. It is probable that the plans were to capture this Confederate regiment, and but for the impetuosity and "previousness" of the scouts in "flushing the cove" before the sportsmen had got the net spread, it would have succeeded.

Soon the scouts returned with jaded horses and without booty and the entire force turned toward Jonesboro, where they arrived after dark.

I learned later that our chief, Captain Duncan, had received orders from General Howard or General Sherman to ride with Kilpatrick's scouts during the day with dispatches from Kilpatrick. At night we were to cut across the country to General Howard's column of infantry, which was on their way toward Macon, on a road twenty miles farther east of the one we were on. This I did not know at the time but supposed we were to go into camp with Griffin's scouts near Jonesboro.

On arriving at their camp, we found the men had camped down promiscuously and it being very dark, we had much trouble passing through and had to be careful lest our horses should tramp on the feet of the tired soldiers lying down. By so doing I got separated from our scouts and followed those of Griffin. There I learned that our scouts had gone farther and undertook to follow them in the dark. After traveling some time in an easterly direction, I discovered a great light to my left and thought it might be the lights of the infantry camps, but after going several miles toward the light and apparently getting no nearer it, I decided that it was Atlanta burning about twenty miles away.[3] I then returned to Griffin's scouts' camp and remained with them three or four days until I had an opportunity to rejoin my own.

3

General Kilpatrick and Lieutenant Griffin

If wars go well, each to a part lays claim;
If ill, then Kings, not subjects, bear the blame.
—Potter

IF ANY OF MY readers can imagine the actions of a "mad Mulla" a "Howling Dervish" or a crazy South Sea Islander while "runnin amuck," they can form a fair opinion of Lieutenant Griffin's actions during an engagement. He seemed to be possessed of absolutely no fear. On the contrary, he acted like a mad bull charging a red flag, apparently realizing no danger and using very poor judgment (as I thought), as to the proper time to strike. This impetuosity led to his death later in the Carolinas.

The route pursued by the cavalry from Jonesboro towards Macon was down one of the beaches of the Flint River. A small force of the enemy was encountered soon after leaving Jonesboro, which caused some delay. They were not sufficiently strong to give us battle, but by repeatedly showing us a bold front and then when about to be attacked, falling back to the next available position for defense, they caused us much annoyance. I think it was on November 17th, when near Griffin, Georgia, at a point where the main road leaves the valley and climbs a long ridge to the table land above, that a force of cavalry with two brass cannon (I think they were twelve pounders) caused considerable annoyance to our advance, delaying it till the main column crowded onto the advance guard.

General Kilpatrick at once got another one of his "tantrums" and ordered a regiment of cavalry to flank them on their (the enemy's) left and then the scouts to follow up a ravine on our left and to "capture the damned things."

An occasional shot was fired from the Confederate artillery from their elevated position, while "Kil" stationed another regiment in their front with instructions to charge as soon as the trap was set. The scouts under Chief Griffin proceeded quietly up the ravine to a point about opposite the artillery. We were perhaps one hundred yards from them, but an almost impenetrable mass of small scrub oak brush intervened. No shots had been fired for several minutes and we began to think they had retreated. The chief had in a whisper ordered us to make our way toward where we supposed the Rebs had been. We had got within eight or ten rods of the battery when one of their guns turned loose again, sending a shell down into the valley below. This shot did the work for Griffin, who could no longer stand this—what would you call it?—still hunt?

He raised the yell and away we went. It was a trick of the scouts in like circumstances for each and every one to raise his voice and give commands as though each commanded a regiment, thus in many instances causing consternation in the enemies' ranks, which if properly followed up, made a victory much more easily attained. In this case the ruse was successful. I think I was about the second or third man who gained the open roadway and at a glance took in the situation. The cannoneers and all, except their captain, had abandoned the guns and ran up the road as soon as we raised the yell, while the captain endeavored frantically to induce them to remain and take off the guns.

Griffin was the only one of our force who carried a saber, and when I pushed into the open, the first thing I saw was Griffin mauling the Reb captain over the back and shoulders with his sword, mop-stick fashion, and calling on him to "Surrender, damn you, surrender."

Our force of scouts was considerably delayed in getting through the brush, hence were showing up in the roadway one at a time. The artillery men who had retreated up the road saw so few "Yanks" coming in, evidently thought they had been duped and began to rally to the rescue of their captain, when, as luck would have it, the regiment of cavalry which had been sent around the enemy's left, at this moment commenced pouring into the road from the opposite side from which we came and the victory was complete.

While, of course, we were not entitled to all of the credit for capturing these two pieces, I think we could be excused for boasting a little of our prowess. It was afterward reported that these pieces were a part of those captured by Hood from Logan on July 22nd.[1] The command then halted for dinner. After a hasty snack, the scouts under Griffin again took the advance and soon came to the table land, which we found to be a beautiful and well-cultivated district, the best we had seen in the state of Georgia. The road here was level and good and the land well cleared and cultivated, we being able to see our way for over a mile. When we arrived at this point, two of the enemy's pickets were seen, who were mounted and were disposed to dally a little with us, retreating only when pushed. This style of warfare did not exactly suit Griffin, so he sounded the yell and started in pursuit at the top of his speed, calling on the boys to follow. As usual the best horses gradually left the slower ones, stringing along the road, each rider trying his best to keep up with his chief.

Here is where my newly captured mare played me false, for instead of keeping along with the largest crowd where I would have preferred to be, she lunged forward keeping well up with the leader. There were two others of the party who also had extra good horses, so we four soon distanced the balance of the scouts, who were, however, using their spurs freely to enable them to be in at the wake.

This road kept nearly parallel but gradually approaching the railroad track, and at a point about a mile from where the race commenced, suddenly turned to the right and crossed the track at a place where the railroad grade cut through a small elevation, making a cut of three or four feet. After crossing the track, the road turned to the left, again keeping parallel to it. At this point the chief was perhaps six rods in advance of me and I, thinking that by following up the railroad track I could recover the lost ground, tried that plan. When I had arrived at a point where I could again get to the road by crossing the rails, I was in the act of doing so when about a hundred Confederate gentlemen who were resting behind a cross fence about one hundred fifty yards away, arose and poured a volley into us that made me wish I was tucked away in my little bed in my mother's chamber. My mare being badly winded, at this instant stumbled and fell. I supposed she was killed, and as those rebellious gentlemen failed to cease firing after the ball was opened, and I then seeing a squadron of perhaps sixty of their mounted partisans filing out from a neighboring lane and coming like a whirlwind toward us, considered that discretion was the better part of valor and immediately adjourned to a young peach orchard nearby. I passed near where Griffin was lying with one leg pinned under his dead horse, but I did not have time to move the previous question. The horses of my other two

companions were lying dead close by and their riders seconded my amend-
ment and joined me in the peach orchard.

This orchard was a sort of nursery of young peach trees, which were perhaps four or five feet high and grew so thick that it made a very good place
of concealment.

While running toward this retreat, it seemed as though the whole Confederate Army was firing at us and that several bushels of bullets were kicking up the dust around us. Fortunately none of us were hit.

The firing ceased when the sortie arrived where our horses lay. I could,
by lying close to the ground, see one of the Rebs trying to assist Griffin to
get his leg out from under his horse, but he was not successful. Another was
trying to lead away my mare which had regained her feet and proved to be
uninjured, but she also proved to one of those obstinate brutes which will
not be led.

Just at this moment Kilpatrick, who had arrived at the head of this plain
a mile away, saw through his glass the true situation and ordered a battery
that was passing to unlimber and shell this squadron of horsemen that was
around us poor scared devils. Never did this sound of shells prove so welcome as at that moment, for it took but two or three to send our Southern
friends scampering down the road and I did not blame them for their haste
for the explosion of those shells was truly invigorating.

The gentleman who was trying to lead away my mare decided that time
was too precious, so he reached over and helped himself to a fine navy revolver that I had attached to the pommel of the saddle, kindly leaving me
the scabbard. It is doubtful if this whole affair lasted more than six minutes,
but at the time it seemed to me to be of an hour's duration.

Later experience convinced me that this affair was a blunder from start
to finish. That it was a trap laid by the "Johns" was plainly evident and
would have been detected by any one of even moderate experience, but
Lieutenant Griffin could not resist the temptation to get up a scrap at every
opportunity. Later in talking with one of his scouts, I was told that he never
did learn discretion but was as eager for fight after dozens of such.

4

Mr. Stokesbury

War is not female province, but the scene
For men: hence; home nor spread mischief here.

OUR SCOUTS' CAMP was located near Monticello. However, it was too early to expect the scouts to come in when I arrived, so to while away the time, I sauntered over into the town. Business was entirely suspended; in fact, that was the state of affairs in about all of the back country towns of the Confederacy. Every day was like Sunday except where there was a portion of the army quartered. Here I made the acquaintance of an old gentleman who informed me that he was one of the enforced refugees from Atlanta, under General Sherman's Order of Expulsion.[1]

I spent the afternoon and evening with him and found him to be an intelligent, agreeable and kindhearted gentleman. I learned from him that he had been for many years a practicing physician in Atlanta. He was at this time about sixty years of age. He was free to converse with me on the war question and spoke very pathetically of the great suffering which necessarily followed the paths of war.

From my recollection the following is a synopsis of the story as told to me by him, as to his former life.

His name was Stokesbury. Previous to the war it had been his custom to take a summer outing each year, sometimes at the Sea Islands at Savannah, at other times in the mountains.

While warmly attached to the cause of the South, he could never in his own mind become convinced that the Confederacy could be successful in establishing its independence.

He was married, had a very pleasant home and a lucrative practice, but was never blessed with a son or daughter, a circumstance which cast a cloud over his otherwise happy home.

In about the year 1852, during one of his visits to Savannah, he became acquainted with a Mr. Stevenson, a retired sea captain. This acquaintance gradually ripened into a warm friendship and many a pleasant day did they spend together in the captain's sloop while coasting along through the many bays and sounds with gun and rod.

On these occasions the doctor often visited the home of his friend, the captain, where he found a bright-eyed little miss of seven or eight years, to whom he became greatly attached. Being then about fifty years of age and having no children of his own, he often begged of the captain and his lady to allow him to adopt the little tot, but this being their only child, it was not to be thought of.

The doctor continued his annual visits to Savannah and the Stevensons until about 1856, when the captain removed to a small town near the coast in South Carolina, where the doctor renewed his visits, never failing to bring some choice presents to his little "Mollie," as he called her.

He stated to me that he thought in all reasonable probability General Sherman would capture Savannah, as by a false military move on the part of General Hood there was not sufficient troops left to cover that city. He said further that in all probability many people would foolishly rush into that city to escape the Yankees.

He especially feared that his friend, Captain Stevenson, would move into Savannah, as it was for many years his home. He then requested as a personal favor that if the fortunes of war should bring me into Savannah, I would inquire after his friend and, if found and he was in straitened circumstances, I would assist him or at least see that he was not unnecessarily oppressed. He gave me directions by which I could learn if the captain was in the city and his whereabouts. Again, if he was not to be found in that city, then if I should ever happen in the neighborhood of his South Carolina home, to call on the family and note their wants, etc.

The doctor spoke with so much pathos that I became interested and promised to look up the Stevensons if possible. He then gave me a short note of introductions, after which I bade him farewell.

About dark the scouts returned; they had given me up, thinking I had taken a pleasure trip down to Andersonville to visit my old friend Captain Wirs.[2] They were glad to learn that Kilpatrick's scouts had assisted in the capture of the artillery.

The next day no event of importance happened worthy of note, but that night after all had retired and fallen asleep, our chief came in and communicated in a low voice the fact that General Howard wished to send a man into Macon in disguise to ascertain the military situation in that city, and called for a volunteer to make the trip. No one responded, as this was out of our line of duty. I think the reward offered was $500, but it may have been larger.

Finally he spoke to the old scout Gillet, saying that he had acquired a great reputation in that line and asked him to undertake the task, which Gillet, finally, after some discussion agreed to do. He was fixed up and started soon after midnight. I did not get to see him before starting, but the next afternoon when we were within a few miles of Macon, we met an old Georgia planter, who was old, fat, hump-backed, and sorry-looking, who was riding a much dilapidated mule with a rope bridle and an old saddle with a broken stirrup on one side and rope on the other. He proved to be Gillet, who told us he had gone to within a couple of miles of Macon and had seen too many troops and too much excitement for his nerves, so he returned. I do not know if he secured the information General Howard wanted, as he was very reticent and did not care to talk much with us about his trip. Neither do I know if he got the reward, but I presume not because none of us received any of the secret service money until we reached Savannah and Gillet had been killed before that time.

I do not remember any event of importance enacted by us until November 22nd.

On that day the left wing under Slocum was aiming for Milledgeville,[3] while the right wing under General Howard was on a road about halfway between Milledgeville and Macon, with several miles intervening and no communication between the two wings.

The scouts were instructed to proceed in a left oblique direction towards Milledgeville and if possible, without exposing ourselves too much, to ascertain the condition of things in that city. We thought perhaps we might see some fun and gain some glory and the scouts were anxious to go.

We left word at the camp for George Matchett, who was absent on some trifling duty and who was expected to return soon, to follow us, and what road we would take. He did return and started to overtake us but by some mischance took a road leading to Gordon and we never saw him alive again. It seems he rode into Gordon several miles ahead of the army thinking to find us there. There was great excitement in the village. Crowds of old and crippled men and discharged Confederate soldiers gathered around, disarmed him, and then a young one-armed soldier just returned from Lee's army stepped toward George saying, "Let me kill another Yank," and deliberately shot him down. If I remember correctly, the citizens stopped the Reb from firing again. I think also that George lived until the advance of the army arrived. These facts were given out by the negroes present. We (the scouts) were informed that the murderer was given a drumhead court martial and shot the next morning at sunrise. My recollection is not clear on the point, and as no history I have ever read mentions the fact, the rumor may be incorrect.

Some six or eight years ago, I met an old soldier who knew Machett's people both before and after the war, and he told me they had never learned what had become of George. I think they lived neat Momence, Illinois.

5

The Demijohn

I covet not, not I, the bad renown
to be the sacker of another's town.

WE OF THE MAIN PARTY, on that day numbering eight, advanced to
within a couple of miles of Milledgeville and prowled—I think that is the
appropriate word—around in hearing of the bells, whistles, and general
confusion incident to the hasty evacuation of the city, trying to learn from
the excited negroes what was going on within.[1]

One of our boys, I think it was Bob,[2] managed by the aid of an accom-
modating darky to unearth a demijohn of an exhilarating fluid that its owner
had undoubtedly secreted from the vandal hands of the bold invaders. Now,
Bob had been known on some previous occasion to indulge rather too freely
in the cup that intoxicates and had become somewhat excited and exhibited a
desire to wipe out the Confederacy without the aid or consent of any person
on earth. So on this occasion the balance of us tried to prevent a recurrence
of this condition by helping him to consume the contents of the demijohn,
in order to save Bob's reputation and prevent him from shocking the dignity
of the governor and legislature of the great state of Georgia, who were then
about to, and in fact were in the act of, abandoning their capital.

I wish to state here that, notwithstanding Bob's love of the flowing
bowl, we, each and all, regarded his judgment as the best in cases, in deter-
mining our actions in all critical emergencies. This attempt on our part had
a contrary effect to that we had anticipated.

About sundown we gained a point about one mile north of the capital
on the high lands overlooking the city. These heights had been fortified for
the city's protection, but the works were now abandoned. From this point
we could see a locomotive and several cars standing at the depot, around

which were soldiers, citizens, women, children, and negroes moving about, apparently in great excitement and confusion.

Now was the time that Bob's demijohn got in its work, for Bob challenged the party to go as far into the town as he would and, as we could not conscientiously abandon him to the mercies of an infuriated foe, followed him slowly into the city. Our march took upon itself a fairly presentable military one until we got into the business part of town. At this point the mayor of the city presented himself, and Captain Duncan demanded the surrender of the city, leaving the impression, without stating it in so many words, that we were backed by the whole of Sherman's army, which was just back there on the hills ready to enforce demand.[3]

He was ready to surrender all right but tried to stipulate that private property should be respected, etc., etc., but Duncan cut him short, saying, "Damn your term, if you don't surrender this city within five minutes, I will signal our people on those hills (pointing to the earthworks), and they will level it with the earth." The mayor replied, "Well, sir, I must submit under protest," and said something else about being overpowered, and the cruelties of war, etc., which I did not fully understand, my attention being called by the return of two or three of our boys who had deployed on other streets and who reported that soldiers and citizens were gathering together in groups and gesticulating as though they were about to resent our intrusion.

As it had been some time since we had interviewed Bob's demijohn, it having been left back on the hills, it did not take much argument to convince us that things were getting too warm for our health, so we gathered up some sixty prisoners and started back in an orderly retreat.

We estimated that there were several hundred Confederate soldiers in town, but none were under arms or in ranks and we did not go nearer than two blocks of the depot where the largest crowds and most of the confusion were, thinking it rather unsafe. All the people appeared to be aware of our presence, but such was the confusion and the surprise, added to the audacity of our move, that no one of them seemed to care to challenge us.

Darkness overtook us before we arrived at the hills and we decided to return to the camp, which we supposed to be eight miles away, with our prisoners. We had not gone more than two miles when in passing through a wide land, which we had passed earlier in the day, we became aware that we were riding into a trap.

On each side of the road was a cornfield of ripe corn, which we remembered to have seen. Our road was blocked by a force of Rebs, the number of which we could only conjecture, but having learned of the presence of a Confederate Cavalry Regiment in the vicinity, we reasoned that this obstacle in our path was that Rebel force. We could hear the tramping of feet and the neighing of horses in our front, but it being very dark, could see nothing. We then retreated a short distance and let down a fence and passed into and through the cornfield to the woods beyond, but in so doing we lost all our prisoners, they having quietly dropped out while passing through the corn.

It was after midnight when we arrived in camp. Our chief made a report of our doings, carefully failing to mention the demijohn episode. However, some of the left wing soldiers who were a little jealous of us got hold of some of the facts and reported them to General Howard, who, in turn, hauled us over the coals rather severely and left a very strong impression on our minds that it had better not occur again; otherwise we might have an opportunity to again tote a knapsack.[4]

In recording this incident of our capture of Milledgeville, General Howard in his reminiscences, published in the *National Tribune*, January 23, 1896, says:

> "Fuller accounts of what we had done had already been forwarded by the hands of Captain Duncan, who had the immediate command of a set of scouts."
>
> Curiously enough this Captain Duncan, who from some reports sent to me about that time by General Blair concerning him and his scouts, appeared to me to be rather reckless, at this time performed a feat quite in keeping with his "SUBSEQUENT REMARKABLE CAREER."
>
> Now, referring to Captain Duncan's enterprise ten miles ahead of us, and toward our left front, I [General Howard] said, "The Mayor of Millegeville surrendered the town, the capital of Georgia, formally to Captain Duncan and a few scouts."

The reader will notice that General Howard makes no mention of Bob's "demijohn" so I presume that Captain Duncan failed to report to him the casus belli of our so-called "remarkable career."

6

Milledgeville

I will not curse thee, ere I learn if yet
Thou relent—if not, all evil blast thee
—Dale

WE LEARNED THAT night that the 14th Corps commanded by General Jeff C. Davis would arrive at Milledgeville at about 10 o'clock A.M. the next day, and, not having yet been admonished by General Howard, we started early and arrived in the city by 8 o'clock. We rode in an orderly manner without the aid of Bob's demijohn.

We found the trains gone, the streets deserted, and a general quietness prevailing. There was nothing to see about the empty streets, nothing to hear or learn, and as plundering was out of our line, we halted at a small public square to await the coming of the army. In a few minutes men, citizens, began to appear here and there and gather into groups, look savagely at us, gesticulate, and run from group to group. While none had arms in sight, we did not doubt that all were as well armed as ourselves.

Not caring to bring on a scrap where there would be no beneficial results, and knowing that help would be at hand soon, we quietly moved over to the state penitentiary, the gates of which were unlocked, and went within, intending to use its walls for our protection in case of attack. Here we found perhaps a dozen negroes and one old Irish sailor, all in the regular stripes. All of the able-bodied prisoners had been released and enlisted in their army a few days previous to this.[1]

Adjacent to the prison walls stood a three-story brick building used as a county or city prison, the upper-story windows overlooking the penitentiary walls. Soon after we arrived in the prison yard, we heard a voice from the third story of the county prison calling on us to release him as he was a Federal soldier. The keys could not be found for some time but at length he was released and reported to us that his name was Henry Conklin,[2] a member of a Michigan Cavalry Regiment and a scout of General Thomas. That he had some twelve months before been sent by Thomas as a spy to the heart of the Confederacy to work disaster to their ammunition manufacturing establishments. He said that he was a graduate of a medical college, had made a special study of chemistry, and by this reason, his ability and knowledge had secured a position as mixer of the ingredients used in manufacturing percussion caps. That he had succeeded in mixing some chemical into the compound that largely destroyed their utility, that the Confederate authorities had become suspicious of him and finally caught him in the act, tried and found him guilty by a military court, and he was then under sentence of death, which sentence was to be executed on return of the papers from Richmond, where they had been sent for approval.

We believed his story at the time and took him in with us as a scout until such time as he could return to his own command. I will say now in passing that we later came to disbelieve his whole story, as he proved to be a notorious liar, a thief, and thoroughly unreliable. That he was a deserter from the Federal army was probable.

Our Irish poet-scout took a special dislike to Conklin and lost no opportunity of ridiculing him. Finally in a well-written poem he nicknamed him "Cotton-gin," a name which clung to him as long as we knew him. The last we saw of Cotton-gin, he was being taken away to Wilmington, N.C., as a prisoner charged with a heinous crime. Before arriving at Savannah we had discovered that the retaining of Conklin as a scout among us would eventually bring us into disrepute, and as we had no direct evidence which would convict him in any court, we simply sent him adrift. He was seen from time to time, generally with some wagon train, where it was believed he was engaged in robbing the citizens as the march proceeded through the Carolinas.

The advance of the 14th Corps arrived on time and we soon left the City of Milledgeville going to Gordon, where we learned of the murder of our comrade, George Matchett.

Some of my readers may wonder how it was that we, being dressed in Rebel uniform, could pass so readily at any time, day or night, to or from any point without being interrupted or arrested. I will state that nearly all the army of the Tennessee soon came to know one or more of us; besides, each of the scouts carried a pass which read as follows:

> Headquarters Department and Army of the Tennessee,
> November 15, 1864
>
> Guards, pickets, patrols and advance guards, pass the bearer
> _____, a special Scout at these Headquarters, at all
> times, for thirty days.
>
> By order of Major General O.O. Howard.
>
> Samuel L. Taggart
> A.A. Gen'l

This pass would be renewed every thirty days, but later it was found not necessary to carry them and some of the boys got a little "squeamish" about the possibility of being captured with such a pass in their pocket; therefore, they were eventually discontinued, except on special occasions. Of course, we were sometimes detained at an outpost where we were not recognized. In such cases it was only necessary for us to ask to be taken to some headquarters nearby where we could be identified.

We had many amusing incidents occur in connection with foragers, who, while away from the main column foraging, were always on the lookout for the grey-coated gentlemen. Occasionally we came upon a party of these "bummers," who did not recognize us and sometimes we were at considerable trouble to be identified.

I remember one occasion when I happened to be alone and came upon a party of foragers who were several miles from their column. They had ordered the negroes of the plantation to prepare for them a sumptuous dinner. The dinner was about ready to be served when I rode up to them. Before any explanations had been made, a young smart alec proposed to disarm me and make me his prisoner. I told him he had better postpone that ceremony until after dinner and invited myself to partake of their feast. One of the men, a sergeant, recognized me and assisted in carrying out the joke by saying, "Certainly, that is but right. It is not fair to take a man prisoner when he is hungry." I was seated by the side of my proposed captor. The sergeant had intimated to the balance my identity and they in turn assisted me in guying the young man. I advised him to eat a hearty dinner as it was probable this was the last good one he would eat for some time. I told him that I had them surrounded by a regiment of Wheeler's cavalry and there was no hope for their rescue. The boys pretended to believe me and commenced filling their pockets with the eatables in sight. The young man, however, had some nerve and did not propose to give up without a fight. He attempted to rise and settle it with me then and there, but the boys talked him out of it, telling him that it would be better for him and all the rest to quietly submit and not have blood on their hands at the eve of certain capture.

After dinner they persuaded me to go to my men and try to induce them not to disturb the foragers, they on their part, agreeing to never, no never, do so anymore. It was fun for the boys but the youngster showed grit just the same.

7

Texas Rangers

At once from every Greek with glad acclaim,
Burst forth the song of war whose lofty notes.

I WISH TO OFFER here a few remarks as to the esteem in which scouts held the leading generals with whom they came in contact.

General Sherman was all business with his subordinates, but was very kind in his treatment of them unless he thought they were exceeding their prerogatives.

I can call to mind an instance when he had given me a verbal order to so-and-so, and my judgment told me that it should be done so-and-so and I replied, "General, if you so order it, I will do so, but if you leave it to me, I shall do it so-and-so," and expected to get fired out of the tent. But much to my surprise he said, "Well, do as you like, but my opinion is so-and-so is the best plan," but events afterward proved that I was right. This scene I shall refer to hereafter. The boys will bear me out in saying it would not have been safe for me to have talked thus to many an understrapper.

With General Howard it was always kindness. Even when he had occasion to censure or reprimand a subordinate, it was done in such language and in such a tone that one felt like it was his kind old father who was censuring him.

Sherman would and did occasionally get on his "high-heeled boots" but Howard, never.

After reaching Gordon, the right wing spent a couple of days destroying the railroad from a point near Macon in an easterly direction to the Oconee River, a distance of twenty-five or thirty miles. Our corps of scouts ranged to the south and southwest, watching the movements of the enemy.[1]

Wheeler had not yet made his appearance but there were a few scattered detachments of Rebels, mostly cavalry, flying hither and thither, approaching as near our columns as was considered safe and picking up an occasional forager.

Among these bands was a part of a brag Texas Regiment of Cavalry, who called themselves "Texas Rangers." I have since learned that there were several of these Texas Cavalry Regiments who denominated themselves "Rangers." If I am not mistaken, this was the 6th Texas Cavalry.

We had run up against several parties of this regiment during the previous week but had managed to hold our own with them. We, however, heard from time to time from the citizens, and especially through the young ladies, that their greatest hopes were to meet Sherman's Scouts, but I cannot say that we lay awake nights reciprocating their desire.

It so happened that while the army was making corkscrews out of railroad iron, that one day, being about twenty-five miles southwest of the army, we learned that a party of seventeen "Johns" were about an hour's travel ahead of us, going in the same direction as ourselves. They were reported to be inquiring for a good place to camp where they could obtain plenty of forage and rations. We held a counsel and decided to try for their capture. As they were not aware that we were following, we had the advantage of them.

We proceeded with good speed but with great caution to overtake them, and at each place we inquired, we got the same story and also learned that we were gaining on them. After thus following for about five miles, we learned that they would certainly camp at the next plantation, a mile distant. We now advanced more cautiously with Joe Bedoll and Jerry Phelan about one hundred yards in advance. When they arrived in sight of the enemy, Joe saw at a glance the true situation, and signaled us in the main body to "move up lively, but quietly," while Jerry dismounted and let down the rail fence.[2] At this moment the Texans saw the two scouts and, supposing them to be of their own command, invited the two to ride over and take supper with them. Then Jerry remounted and the two rode toward the Texans at a walk, the distance being about a hundred yards. When they had gained about two-thirds of the distance, our main body appeared at the entrance of the field, when on sight of us the Texans took the alarm, and started for their arms but they were too late, for the advance raised the yell and charged, getting between them and their arms. Jerry's horse being a good vaulter and fence being low, he jumped into the stock-lot. I doubt if thirty seconds transpired before the main body were at their elbows supporting them.

Two of the Texans succeeded in gaining the swamp beyond; the balance, fifteen, surrendered at discretion.

When the advance raised the yell, it was answered by the balance with interest, the Texans telling us afterwards they thought a regiment, at least, had them surrounded. The whole thing lasted so short a time that a person had no time to think. In this capture we got fifteen prisoners, including the lieutenant commanding the squadron, seventeen good horses, a few carbines, and about twenty fine revolvers.

Knowing that the country was full of Rebs, we lost no time in hiking out for our command, it being midnight before we reached it. The Texans, when they learned the truth, were very much crestfallen. The lieutenant remarked that he did not care so much for being captured, as the fact of being taken by so small a force, and said, "Boys, I'll just give you'ns a hundred dollars if you'ns will not tell this part of the story." In the long ride that night, we had a good visit with our captives and found them very sociable fellows, but we took care that they did not turn the tables on us.

It is in order to state here that on this occasion Bob did not have his demijohn along.

This capture supplied us with a surplus of horses from which the field officers were generously supplied.

It had become an unwritten law, rigidly adhered to by both Federal and Confederates, that all horses, arms, and equipment captured by any soldier or squad belonged to the captors, and were scarcely ever turned over to the quartermaster.

For a long time the boys in boasting of their brilliant deeds never forgot to mention the capture of the proud Texans.

Some of the experiences of the scouts were almost incredible, even to those who were marching in the ranks of the columns going to "the Sea."

I remember in 1866 visiting a friend who had been a playmate before the war and who was a soldier on this same march, and good one, too. His mother had been like a mother to me in the old days, and she, having read many of my doings in the state papers, kept me up till near midnight telling of some of our adventures, and I pledge my word that I told nothing but the truth, without coloring it in the least. Ed (my friend and comrade) sat and listened with the rest, but when he and I had gone to bed, said, "George, what made you tell such damned big lies?" Thus it was that those in ranks could form no correct ideas of our experiences and adventures, especially if Bob had his demijohn with us. General Howard would occasionally get an inkling of it and then we would get a lecture. I think he would long ago have sent us back to our old commands but for the fact that whatever he sent us to do was accomplished if within the power of man, and he no doubt thought with President Lincoln, that, "It is poor policy to swap horses while crossing a stream."

8

Texans Again

Who dares think one thing and another tell
My heart detests him as the gates of hell.
—*Iliad*

THE NEXT DAY WE rode over the same route of the preceding one. Among us were two scouts who were not with us on the previous day, and we took pleasure in showing them just how we played it on the Texans, pointing out the ground, etc. Soon after passing the site of the capture, we learned of another party of Texans who were ahead of us pursuing the same direction. By this time we had become very egotistic and thought we could accomplish almost anything we undertook, so we started out to repeat the trick of the day before. We had followed them perhaps six or seven miles, when at about noon we came to a fine plantation house with the lady and several negroes standing at the front gate. We knew that we were hot on the trail and close to the enemy and did not have time to palaver with the lady. The main body had halted a moment at the gate to make inquiries, when the lady said (probably taking us for Confederates), "Now gentlemen, I want you to alight and have your horses fed and I will have a good dinner for you. I have never had an opportunity to entertain any of our soldiers and now you are all going away and the Yankees will be upon us and I will never again have a chance to do so." Then turning to the negroes, said, "Jane, you and Liddy go and catch some chickens and—" But we heard no more, for at that moment we saw Pat Wallace and Bob coming from the front at a gallop who signaled us to "get out of this and quick, too." They had seen a large party of Rebs closing in on us and were just in time to prevent our capture.

As we turned to retreat, we saw a well-dressed Rebel officer who had ridden into the main road from a side road about a hundred yards in our rear. He was standing looking at us but I could see no arms. I started for him at a gallop, asking the boys to lag behind and let me handle him alone. He showed a disposition to skedaddle but, apparently judging that I was the best mounted, hesitated and let me approach, and surrendered on demand. I got from him a pair of silver spurs and a field glass. He would not tell his rank or residence but sullenly submitted. He must have been a field officer of this Texas Regiment.

Instead of retreating along the main road, we turned into the byroad that the officer had come in on and made good time for a mile or more, when we came to a pond of water in the road from recent rains. It was belly-deep to the horses and almost twelve rods across.

Amick and I, who were in advance, had got across and up to a sharp angle in the road and were just in the act of turning the angle when a shot came from our right front. Amick was probably a few inches in advance of me. The bullet passed in front of me and cut the back of his coat wide open. I thought for an instant that he was killed. We looked up the road from where the shot was fired and saw perhaps twenty or thirty horses standing in a bunch about a hundred yards away, but saw no men. An ambush was our first thought and we started back at a gallop. The main body were then in the pond and I want to say that we got out of there pretty lively. So rapid was our movement that we forgot to save our prisoner, who deliberately rode over to his friends. He refused to accompany us and we could not shoot him in cold blood, but I had his glass and spurs all right.

As the enemy was in front of us and a large force to the rear of us, we had nothing to do but take to the woods, where we made a circuit of three or four miles and arrived on a road to the rear of those who had fired on us. There we halted a few moments at a house where the lady told us that a party of two Texans had passed there two hours before, gathering up and confiscating all the horses and mules worth taking. They had taken all hers and besides had taken one of her negroes to help lead them. While we were there, the negro came up nearly out of breath and reported to us that he was with the party who fired at Amick and me—that they had heard the splashing of our horses through the water and had dismounted to await results. Seeing but two of us, one of them fired the shot, then both took to their heels through the woods, leaving the negro and horses to shift for themselves. The negro had then also left the horses and hiked for home.

I want to say right here that afterward when we told of our exploits, we always forgot to mention the fact that we were stampeded by two men who were trying their level best to get away from us.

We learned here also that we were in the midst of a large force of Confederates who were deployed along all the roads, confiscating all the horses and mules they could find. This knowledge prevented us from stopping for dinner in that neighborhood.

We then traveled slowly, most of the time through the woods, till nearly dark, at which time we reasoned that we were far enough from the Rebel force to justify us in hunting for something to eat and some horse feed. In the meantime we had arrived in a much poorer country, where the roads and houses were few and far between. It was a very dark and cloudy night and it was with difficulty that we could find our way. About nine o'clock a light was discovered some distance off the road and we went to it, where we found a house of the poorer order. There were five or six women who had been, during the day, engaged in killing and dressing hogs, with perhaps the aid of some man who was hiding out from the conscripting officers, at least that was the way we sized up the situation. No man, however, except an old negro was seen about the place. We inquired if we could get some supper and horse feed and, being answered in the affirmative, fed our horses and, stationing the aged negro as a guard to notify us of the approach of anyone, went in to supper. It was evident that they had prepared a supper for themselves according to the custom prevailing in the South among the poorer classes at a hog-killing, that is, had boiled the jowls of the hog and prepared the chittlings. This with those people was regarded as a great treat. We were seated on a long bench on either side of a long, rough board table, with one dim light made by a cotton rag in an old cracked saucer, on which some of the hog's fat was larded.

This supper proved very palatable to us hungry scouts, until Amick, who sat by my side, happened to get a hard substance in his mouth, and taking it out to look at it, found it to closely resemble a human tooth. He passed it to me for my inspection and I passed it to others, who all pronounced the same. It is sufficient to say that our appetites were at once appeased and our supper concluded. We arose at once and, looking at the poorly clad, frightened women in the dim light, were reminded of the witches of Macbeth.

After handing them a $100 Confederate bill, we took our departure, and not till sometime afterward did it occur to us that the objectionable masticator was that of one of the razorbacks, slaughtered on that day.

We did not return to camp that night but lodged in a corn shed found at the next plantation.

9

Missouri Jayhawkers

Judges, rise
Assume the pebbles, and decide the cause,
Your oath revering.

NEXT MORNING WE divided our forces into three or four squads and advanced on different roads toward the column of troops. About noon Amick and I (who traveled together) arrived at a house where two foragers had been and had appropriated some ham and chickens, but had passed on to the next plantation. A young lady stood on the porch and recognizing us as Confederates came running out to tell us of the terrible doings of the Yankees. They had taken two of the best hams in the smokehouse and the best hen on the place, "Old Speck." We consoled her as much as we could and expressed a wish that we had been there to get a chance at those Yankees, etc., etc. She invited us to stay for dinner, an invitation we were fishing for, and we accepted readily. The conversation on her part during dinner was about the "terrible atrocities of the invaders." She seemed especially worried because the two Yankees had gone on toward her "Grandpa's." While she was bidding us adieu, she looked up the road and saw the foragers returning, one of them mounted on an old grey mare, and exclaimed, "There they come now and they have got Grandma's old Dolly, kill them." The foragers advanced toward us unconcernedly, apparently thinking we were Federals, but because of our grey clothes had no reason for so thinking. The horse and men were so loaded down with hams, chickens, and turkeys that they could not very well handle their guns. They came up to the gate where Amick and the young lady stood. Amick pulled a gun and demanded their surrender, which they did without a word of protest.

While he kept them covered, I stepped forward and relieved them of their arms, when the lady said, "Now, why don't you kill them?" We told her that we had special orders to take such men when captured to headquarters, together with their plunder to be used as evidence against them, where they would be tried and shot.

This seemed to satisfy her and we started off with our "prisoners." They were a sickly looking pair of foragers. When we got out of sight of the plantation and told them the truth, returning their guns, we told them to be more careful in the future about walking deliberately up to a party of grey-coated gentlemen.

These men must have been new recruits; old soldiers would not have been thus caught.

This was the first time I had heard a lady use such cruel and murderous language. I firmly believe that if we had given her a gun, she would have killed them both.

The following day the scouts went to the Oconee River and found a crossing a few miles below Balls Ferry. It was in the woods on a private road where some planters had provided a private ferry boat, no house being in sight. The small ferry boat was at the opposite side of the river, so Dawson swam his horse across and brought the boat back to us. Our saddles were removed to the boat and we swam the horses alongside and thus effected a crossing. After ranging about for some time and finding nothing worthy of reporting, we returned to the ferry and found the boat gone, so each one had to swim his horse. This was my first experience in riding a horse while swimming—but as Bob had found another demijohn that afternoon, we did not get very wet—at least that was the general opinion. It was dark when we got across, and in returning to Balls Ferry, to where our headquarters had moved, we came across the 29th Missouri Mounted Infantry, who were encamped at a plantation where there was an abundance of forage. As we were not in exactly the condition in which we would like to be when returning to our own camp, where we were liable to meet General Howard, we invited ourselves to camp with the Missouri Jayhawkers. With some grumbling on their part, we were permitted to remain. The next morning we awoke very late to discover that the Jayhawkers were gone and with them every revolver, saddle, and hat belonging to our party. They had kindly left us our horses. Then the main question was to secure substitutes without the story getting out. We were not afraid the Missouri boys would give it away until the story should become old.

Fortunately for me I learned that my old regiment, the 32nd Wisconsin, was in camp nearby, so I sneaked in and secured an old hat from my old bunk-mate, John White, and old saddle from our regimental quartermaster and a revolver from the commissary sergeant. In time, the other boys fared about as well, but we failed to show up at our own quarters till night, when we had a cock and bull story to account for our delay.

Had General Howard been aware of our conduct on this and other similar occasions, it is safe to say that we would each and all have been sent back to our old commands to trudge through the mud on foot, and our chance to distinguish ourselves would have been forever lost.

The quality of liquor that Bob was most partial to was a blackberry wine, made in large quantities by and for the ladies. This would be called by old toppers a very mild beverage, but large quantities produced great effects, especially with Bob.

IO

Peach Wine

And nothing doth is help or profit as
Gaining fair fame, a shameful death to die.
—Plumptre

THE PONTOON BRIDGE being ready, we crossed over the river the next morning ahead of the army and went some thirty miles in a right oblique direction. We saw none of the enemy nor heard of any. We stopped about the middle of the afternoon at a fine and wealthy plantation. The only white people present were the madam and a grown daughter, but there were more than a hundred negroes. Of course, the negroes were not expected to work in the fields so near an approach of the Yankees, so all were about the plantation houses.

We were kindly treated, our horses being fed and Captain Duncan and Sergeant Amick (both being what are called "ladies' men"), were being entertained in the parlor by the ladies. The captain being a fine musician, we on the outside soon heard a piano with his voice, accompanied by that of a lady's, in melodies that were kept up the better part of the afternoon. Amick, who sat there listening to the conversation of the madam, heard, or imagined that he heard, something unusual going on outside and wanted to investigate, but being fearful that if he attempted to do so, it might "bust up the séance."

What was going on outside was this: Bob, who had a keen nose for the distilled juice of the peach, had induced or intimidated the negro mammy who presided over the kitchen to purloin a certain wicker-covered glass vessel of the capacity of about twelve quarts from her mistress's store room. Soon the music from the parlor became sweeter than ever and Bob got one of his "funny streaks."

All of Sherman's "bummers" and many other "bummers" will remember the rumor circulated throughout the army that the Rebel authorities had adopted the practice of chasing escaped Yankee prisoners with blood hounds, and that an order had been issued by someone in authority on our side to "kill all blood hounds."[1]

Now, Bob didn't like a dog "no how." All dogs were alike to him. He had taken up a position behind the smokehouse on a beautiful lawn with the demijohn by his side and was being entertained by several young negroes, whom he had caused to dance. All the balance of the darkies as well as all the dogs of the plantation had formed a circle around the dancers and were enjoying the scene as well.

Suddenly a new idea occurred to Bob. He interviewed the demijohn again and then pulled out a revolver and ordered all the negroes to stand still until he could talk to them, on pain of instant death. They obeyed and Bob spoke to them about as follows: "Dogs are bad things. Dogs frequently bite people. I am afraid of dogs. Now I want each of you to catch a dog— don't let any get away. Hold them till I give you further orders." Then when all the dogs were secured, he noticed a large stone on the lawn where it had been used for cracking nuts. He then said, "I'll kill the first nigger that lets his dog get away." Then he caused them, one at a time, to bring their dogs up and lay their heads on the stone, where he soon ended its existence by a blow from an axe.

As fast as they were killed, he caused them to be thrown into a pile, and had got nearly through with his task when the madam came tearing and screaming at the top of her lungs, followed by Amick and the captain. The captain berated Bob soundly, but I thought I could not detect much venom in his "cussing."

The smile on Amick's face was beautiful to behold. By actual count, there were over forty dogs in the pile.

I have always thought that out of this grew the story told by General Grant in his *Memoirs*, in Volume II, page 364.[2]

We lost a good supper on account of this funny business of Bob's, but it afforded us many a hearty laugh.

It might be thought a very risky piece of business to act thus in the enemy's country—but we always provided against surprises by stationing negroes in all possible directions to alarm us in case of the approach of strangers, and when our horses were being fed, a negro was always required to stand beside each one with the bridle in hand ready to slip the bits between the horse's teeth at the slightest alarm, and they were always faithful to the trust.

Furthermore we had one scout, Joe Bedoll, who enjoyed a good drink of peach juice as well as any man I ever saw, but Joe could not by any means be induced to partake of the flowing bowl when away from camp. The only bad results ever experienced by us on account of overindulgence was that in case of a scrap: it had a tendency to give us too much "Dutch" courage.

Joe would never take chances on our security but saw to it personally that all precautions had been taken.

The scouts were not controlled by ordinary military rules. There was no detailing of guards, nothing of that sort. If anything was to be done, all were willing to do it without being told, and if any were not willing, they were soon relieved and returned to their former regiment.

Captain Duncan was what the world would call a gentleman. He was of Scottish birth, well educated, well bred, well built, with a slight but pleasant Scotch accent, good judgment, and had all that goes toward making a good man, but the scouts came to believe that at least half their number was his equal as a scout.

This caused no friction, however, nor was there any occasion for friction. In camp, if Captain Duncan was present, he was the intermediary to carry reports and bring orders from the generals. If he was not present, some other scout filled the place equally well. There is, however, no doubt but that his conservatism kept us out of many bad scrapes.

The next day I did not ride with the force but they returned late at night, having had a set-to with a portion of Wheeler's men and brought in one of Wheeler's prominent scouts as a prisoner. This man we knew by reputation and name (I have forgotten the name). He was a very intelligent and sociable man and enjoyed a good breakfast with us, after which he was turned over to the Provost marshal, but escaped the following night. We had intended to see that he was well provided with comforts, but he saw it in another light.

II

Ferry

He, too, has fallen. Lo! In one brief word
I tell thee all: War never, with good will
Doth choose the evil man, or leave the good.
—*Iliad*

ABOUT NOVEMBER 30th, General Howard ordered the scouts to cut loose from the column and proceed rapidly toward Millen, cross the Ogeechee River above the town, and ascertain if the many thousands of prisoners held there had been removed.[1] If not sent away, we were ordered to get beyond the town and destroy as many railroad bridges as possible to prevent their being removed, then retire to the woods and swamps, there to remain until the army came up. That night we arrived within one mile of the river at a point twelve to fifteen miles above Millen. We had met no Confederates during the day and camped at a small plantation house, where we occupied soft beds once more. That night Dawson and Wallace went down to the river, where there was a neighborhood ferry but no houses. The river was nearly bank full and running rapidly. It being quite dark, they could only see dimly the outlines of the ferry boat and a white horse on the opposite bank. They could also hear some men paddling or bailing out a skiff. They fired at random, which fire was returned, killing Dawson's horse.

This was a mistake; no shots should have been fired. The enemy should have been permitted to remain in ignorance of our presence. The boys soon returned, Dawson carrying his saddle back to the house, where he rustled another horse. The next morning after an early breakfast, we started for the ferry. When we had proceeded about half a mile, Joe Bedoll discovered that he had left a fine revolver under his pillow and asked us to wait for him while he recovered it. In a few minutes we heard firing in the direction of our last night's camp. Soon, Joe made his appearance in the distance coming at a gallop. He signaled us to lay a trap, which we at once did. Joe passed down through us as though he had important and pressing business at the front. He was followed closely by two well-dressed and dudish-looking Texans, who were pumping lead at him at every opportunity.

Shooting from a horse back while running is not considered very dangerous to the man fired at and Joe had a big grin on his face as he passed us. The dudes gracefully surrendered when they had to, or fare worse.

We then proceeded to the ferry with our prisoners, where we found things just as the boys had left them the night before, except that the skiff was gone. The ferry boat was on the other side, where there were also four horses tied to trees. They were saddled and had apparently been there all night. There was a small breastwork thrown up across the road but we could see no men. Things looked rather suspicious. We had reason to think that a force of Rebs was concealed in the breastworks, only awaiting our arrival to capture or kill us. We tried all sorts of schemes to determine if the works were occupied, without success. Chief Duncan then challenged me to swim over and get the ferry boat, but I frankly confessed that I did not have sand enough to try it. I had a large clumsy horse that was a poor swimmer and the current was fearful; those breastworks only twelve rods away did not look particularly enticing. Then Amick started across but his horse turned with him and he was so loaded down with revolvers that we had difficulty in rescuing him. Then little Dawson stripped himself of all surplus weight and, having a fine swimming horse, succeeded in getting across. We had all dismounted and taken position where we could command the works. Dawson walked up to the breastworks and found them empty.

It was then evident to us that this was an advance picket post of the enemy, whose duty it was to watch the ferry in anticipation of the advance of Sherman's army. Believing that a large force had arrived, and being home guards themselves without much experience in warfare, they had abandoned everything, gone back to their reserves, and reported that the Yankees were coming in force.

Dawson, of course, had the first choice of the captured horses. We were ferried over and marched back from the river slowly, looking out for the enemy. We soon arrived at a large plantation. The buildings stood on a slight rise of ground near the center of a field of, perhaps, three hundred acres, all being in one field that had no cross fences. The road entered through a big gate on one side and went out at the opposite side through another one.

When we arrived opposite the plantation house, an old negro came out to us and, taking off his hat and pointing to the opposite gate, said: "For de Lord's sake don't go up dare, dare is more dan a million of our folks up dare."

Right here I must explain a matter that had been bothering us all the morning. It was known to us that General Sherman had sent the 29th Missouri Mounted Infantry by another route to perform the same duty assigned to us. A part of our force was of the opinion that the force ahead of us was none other than that regiment, who supposing us to be Rebels, had laid a little trap for us. The balance were of a different opinion. We discussed the matter pro and con and cross-questioned the negro so much that he began to think he had made a mistake in supposing us to be Yankees, and got so confused in his replies that we could arrive at no definite conclusion. Finally he became so rattled that he was not sure that the "million of our folks" spoken of had been there since last night. Gillet and I riding in advance, we then started up toward the farther gate feeling reasonably safe. Now, it has been characteristic of me all my life in arguing a point, that I could never recall the clinching argument at a time when it would be most effective, but when too late I could do so. So in this case I had taken a part in the discussion as to what force this really was, but could not at the time think of my clinching reason, but when we (the advance) had reached a point about one hundred yards of the gate, and no one in sight in front of us, this clincher occurred to me, and I stopped my horse to speak with those in the rear, but I never finished the argument.

The Rebs, for such they proved to be, seeing me stop, supposed I had discovered them and arose from behind the fence and all demanding, "Surrender, you damned Yankees, surrender!" Of course, we halted, except our two prisoners, who kept on toward the gate. They were dressed in the same uniform we were and it was reasonable to suppose that they were members of our party who had gone forward to arrange for our surrender. We scouts hastily gathered into a group and discussed the question as to what was best to do. Some were in favor of surrendering while others said that the chances were equal of our being killed or escaping, besides we had just received, and had with us, our passes, and some of the boys thought it would be bad policy to be captured with those in our possession. In the meantime, the Rebs were calling out in a hundred voices, "Surrender! Surrender! Surrender!" Just then one of the boys, I think it was Jim Taylor, made a break for the rear with a yell. We knew then that the whole line of the enemy would turn loose on us and concluded we might as well take our chances running as standing, so all started with a yell. Immediately they did turn loose and it seemed as though our weight in lead was being sent after us. Taylor was hit in the arm. Smith got one through the side, and Gillet through the heart. Several horses were hit but managed to take us beyond the deadline. The Rebs having all fired at once, we got beyond their range before they could reload. They must have reasoned that we were the advance of a large force because they did not attempt to pursue us.[2]

We retreated to the ferry, where we found the 29th Missouri, who had heard the volley and came in on a road parallel to the river. Explanations followed and the 29th went back towards the Rebs to engage or monkey with them. Part of our force of scouts accompanied them, while Amick and I were detached to go across the ferry and go down the opposite side of the river and to try to reach Millen from that direction, to obey our instructions about the destruction of railroad bridges, etc.

12

Millen

And from the fenny land,
Came dripping the chill dews, rotting our clothes,
Matting our hair, like hides of shaggy beasts.

WE FOUND NO Confederate force on the south side of the Ogeechee River and arrived about dark at a point about four miles off the river and opposite a bridge which crossed it something like a mile above Millen. There we found a bright young negro who was well acquainted with all the roads in the vicinity, who reported that it would be better, if possible, to cross on the bridge at this point, as there was no other suitable one to be found for many miles below. That the river bottoms grew wider and at this season of the year the swamps and lowlands were flooded and impassable.

After supper and a rest we took the negro as a guide and he led us toward the bridge. We found on approaching the river that the road had been built up above the overflow on a sort of trestle, three or four feet high and well planked for a distance of nearly half a mile before reaching the river. The bottoms were generally overflowed, with here and there a dry hummock of half an acre. It was a clear, still, cool night—one of those nights when one can hear a slight sound a long distance. It seemed to me that the people of Savannah should be able hear the noise of our horses' feet on those planks.

Our guide had reported to us that on the previous day there had been no guards at the bridge. When we arrived there about midnight, we found no guards at the bridge—it had been burned that afternoon—so we had to return to dry land. Imagine our surprise when we had got halfway back on this causeway to find a few planks removed at a point near one of the hummocks spoken of.

We were then in a quandary as to what to do. If it was a trap, our only chance was to run for it. We could not remain where we were nor could we take to the woods because the woods were full of water and alligators. There was some moonlight, we could see fairly well, so we ordered the guide to replace the planks while we guarded him from attack, then to move on slowly for a short distance and await us. When all was ready, we ran the gauntlet at full speed. Much to our surprise and satisfaction, no shots were fired and we never did discover the cause of the "trap" as we called it.

On reaching dry land, we held a council and the guide told us of a way to reach the town in a dugout by following the overflowed swamps and lagoons. He explained the route by saying that it was the way the plantation negroes visited their sweethearts in the town at night when it was necessary to avoid the patrols.

For the benefit of those of my readers who are not familiar with the customs of the South in antebellum days, I will state that it was the rule for young men, sons of the planters, to form themselves into patrols of two or three men, who would ride along the principal roads at night, to see if any of the blacks were prowling about, away from their quarters. If any were found without a pass and failed to give a good account of themselves, they received a good thrashing then and there. During the war when the young men were away in the army, the home guards, consisting of old men and boys under sixteen years, performed this service.

We then retired to the outskirts of a plantation where we concealed our horses and our guide procured some bread and meat for us for the trip. We had promised the guide $500.00 in Confederate money to see us through, and another negro $100.00 to care for our horses until our return, let the time be long or short. He was to take them into the overflow to one of those hummocks where he was to visit and feed them once a day, all of which was faithfully performed by both parties to the contract. Confederate money would still purchase some things at an enormous price, even after the army had passed, but we never omitted to tell the parties of negroes or poor whites to whom we paid it to buy something of permanent value with it as soon as possible, as it would soon be entirely worthless.

Our guide secured a good dugout that the plantation negroes had made and concealed, and we paddled down the swamps and lagoons, the guide steering the course between the cypress trees, which grew so thick that we could never have gotten through, even if we had known the route, without his help. At length about daybreak, we emerged from the mouth of a lagoon into the river, just a little below the town. At this point there was no over-flowed land on the north side of the river, so we pulled the canoe into the brush and crept on our hands and knees through to the cleared land where we could see the town, three or four hundred yards away.

We could see a man on the depot platform whom our guide recognized as an inhabitant of the town. We could also see several other men walking about as though waiting for something. Most of them wore the Confederate uniform.

If we should learn that the prisoners were removed, we would have nothing more to do, but were they removed?[1] That was the question. It would not do for us to go into town to inquire; there were not outlying plantations at which we could learn the facts. The only solution was to send our guide into town to ascertain, which plan we adopted.

From where we were, we could see much that was going on, but the distance was such that we could not form correct conclusions. It was like watching the motions of deaf and dumb people talking with their fingers. We saw our guide go strolling lazily along like the average plantation darky, as if he was hunting the kitchen of some black mammy where he could get a snack. When opposite the depot we saw him stop and slowly approach the man on the platform, where they appeared to engage in an earnest conversation, the negro occasionally extending his arm in our direction, and we began to fear that he was turning traitor to us, giving us away, and we decided that if worst came to worst, we would retreat to a dense thicket and hold out, if possible, till the army came. However, the negro soon strolled leisurely uptown, and as far as we could see him, he seemed unconcerned and indifferent as to his future actions. About noon he returned to us from an entirely different direction and reported to us that the prisoners had been removed two days previous and the only Confederate force in town was one company cavalry, who were keeping a sharp lookout from the direction up the river. We had nothing further to do now than to await the arrival of the army.

This was on December 2, 1864, as history tells us, but as I kept no diary, I have to depend on history for dates.

Toward evening we began to hear occasional cannonading and other sounds incident to the approach of an army, and also noticed that the people had entirely disappeared from the streets of Millen, so we crept along the riverfront toward the destroyed bridge above the town, carefully avoiding the town for fear that some lurking Rebs might give us trouble. Not having our horses with us, we were not looking for a scrap. We arrived at the site of the bridge after dark and found it occupied by a strong picket, and our pontooners were building a pontoon bridge across the river near the site of the destroyed one. Apparently not believing us, the pickets were disposed to keep us with them till morning (we having destroyed our passes), but after some pretty plain talk with the officer in charge, he consented to send us under guard to General Howard's tent, where we found him not far from where we had left our horses. These guards had taken charge of our arms also and it was after much persuasion that they consented to take them along. We could hear them congratulating themselves on having made a capture and that they would each be enriched by a fine revolver.

When we arrived at headquarters, we found the general up, and on sight of us, he took in the situation at once, and said: "Ah ha, you are the gentlemen I have been wanting to see for some time," then telling the sergeant in charge that he would take care of us, they started away, but on being informed that the guard had our weapons, he called them back and told the sergeant that he would take charge of our weapons also. I saw a crestfallen look on the sergeant's face as he delivered them up.

We here recovered our horses and rejoined our comrades, who were snoozing in their quarters, where we took some much-needed rest and sleep.

13

Pine Cones

I know that I am a man, and I can count
No more than thou, on what tomorrow brings.

FROM MILLEN, GENERAL Howard's headquarters and the 15th Corps remained on the south side of the Ogeechee river, while the 17th Corps crossed to the north side, both corps following down and parallel to the river.

Of course, communication was kept up between the two columns by means of the scouts, and an occasional staff office who accompanied them.

For ten days past we had been hearing the citizens speak of the low country, which they called the "wire grass" country.[1] We had now reached a section that was unmistakably the one referred to. The country was nearly a dead level with open pine woods. There was scarcely any undergrowth or down timber so that teams could be driven anywhere without obstructions. The trees were generally some distance apart so that one could see long distances. The land was quite poor and the only vegetation in the woods being a sparse growth of species of grass, which was called wire grass and which well deserved the name. It was of the consistency of broom wire and no animals except a horse or mule would or could eat it, while even these would grow poor on it. The houses were few and far between and these only of the poorer classes. The land and people were so poor, forage and food were becoming scarce. The army was now about seventy miles from Savannah and fifty from King's Bridge, which crossed the Ogeechee nearly due south of Savannah.

The scouts often had occasion to cross lines of troops, and while few know our names, many knew who we were and our occupation. For some reason the soldiers had got it into their heads that the scouts were omnipresent and omniscient. Whenever we came in contact with our troops who recognized us, they would fire questions at us in such profusion that we were glad to get away. The burden of their queries was, "Where are we going?" Even line officers were not averse to asking us, confidentially, where the terminus of the great march was to be, as though they thought we were in a better position to know than they, when, as a matter of fact, it is doubtful if twenty men in the entire army knew. The principal conversation in the ranks was speculation as to our final destination and purpose. Some would have it that we were simply trying to decoy Hood away from Nashville; others that we were keeping up the appearance of aiming for Augusta to call off the Confederate troops from points farther south, that we then would swing around and make a sudden dash for Mobile. Still others insisted that we were marching "On to Richmond" to relieve General Grant from his dilemma.

Whatever the destination might be, all seemed to be confident of their ability to accomplish whatever "Uncle Billy" might plan. I wish here to mention a fact that all historians and writers have ignored, and one which every soldier who "Marched to the Sea" will remember.

The pine trees growing in the wire grass region were of the variety known as the long leafed pine, leaves or spines of which were on average of sixteen inches in length. The burrs, or cones, of this variety are of enormous size, and during the fall and winter months lay under the trees in wagon loads. These burrs are very tough and elastic. When the army arrived at the Pine Belt, these cones were just beginning to fall and were a great curiosity to those who had never before seen them.

The marches were easy and the men strong and full of life and vim. At first a man would kick one of the cones lying in the road; the cone, of course, would be sent forward through the ranks, then another soldier would give it another kick, which being repeated the cone in question would travel more than twice as fast as the column. Then another plan was adopted to pass the time and amuse the solders. Each would select a cone which he called his own which he would give a slight kick, then when he overtook it would again kick, and repeat, each trying to see who could take theirs along the farthest. I have heard soldiers claim to have kicked their cones along a whole day's march, a distance of fifteen miles, then save it up for the next day's kicking. It was a common sight to see, on arriving at Savannah, thousands of soldiers with the toes of their shoes kicked out.

Quite a force of Rebs remained in our front and on our right flank, on the south side of the river; their principal duty appeared to be to watch our movements and gather up all the horses and mules for their use and to prevent us from getting them. This made the few citizens very sore towards them, saying they expected this treatment from the Yankees but not from those who claimed to be their friends.

The first day out from Millen, the scouts had gained a point twenty or more miles in a southeasterly direction, when we came to a plantation of rather better appearance than any we had seen for some time. The old gentleman who was at home said that the Confederates had that day taken all his horses and mules, but an old darky on the place told us a different story. He said that the horses were in a swamp thicket about five miles away, and that among them was a fine stallion "wuth five hun'd dollas." This was sufficient to whet the appetite of Captain Duncan, who at this time happened to be in want of a good horse, so after getting a good description of the place of concealment, we pursued our course. When we arrived at a point within a mile of where the horses were, Bedoll and I were left on the main road as sort of picket while the rest went for the stock. Joe and I dismounted in the open pine woods and waited an unusual length of time for the party to return. Suddenly we espied a mounted Reb approaching us from our front. We waited quietly for him, but when he had got to within about forty rods of us, he saw us and halted. We tried by signals and hallooing to get him to join us but he seem wary and suspicious and would come but a few steps at a time, then call out to inquire who we were. Now, one of our scouts had some time previously been a prisoner for a few days in the custody of the 6th Georgia Cavalry and had learned and remembered the names of several of the officers. We had often used this knowledge to some purpose. On many occasions when we would come up with one of the Rebs, by leading him to believe that we belonged to the 6th Georgia, we would obtain valuable information that might have taken us days to secure by other methods.

Joe asked me to remain behind so he could interview Mr. John, but Mr. John did not seem to want to become too close an acquaintance. He would retreat a short distance when Joe would step out and palaver with him gradually approaching. This movement was repeated several times until Joe got within one hundred yards of him, when Mr. John became convinced that "Joe was no friend of his" and skipped out for his rear. Joe, having an exceedingly good horse, followed him, firing and demanding him to halt and surrender but Mr. John did not halt "worth a cent." On the contrary he led the way up a lane which led into a main road, which ran at right angles to it. Joe was close to him when they got near the junction of the land and main road, when all at once he found himself in the midst of two or three companies of Rebel cavalry. They were on both sides of the road and could not fire at Joe without endangering their men on the opposite side; besides they thought they had him in a bag and did not need to fire. Joe found that he was in for it. He could not retreat so he kept on, and when he got to the farther end of the lane, he saw on the opposite side of the road a low fence with a dense peach orchard beyond, and as the road to the right and left were filled with men and horses, he kept straight on, jumped his horse over the fence, and hiked out for the woods. The Rebs fired a volley at him but fortunately hit neither him nor the horse. He soon distanced his pursuers and, by making a great circuit, joined our party a couple of hours later.

When Joe started on his charge, I, of course, started as fast as I could to follow, but being some distance in the rear, I was just in the act of entering the lane when the yelling and firing at him brought me to a sudden halt. Seeing a large force at the farther end of the lane, I concluded I could give Joe no assistance and retreated to the junction of the roads where our party had left us and where I found them. They had just arrived, having heard the firing at Joe. Captain Duncan had secured his fine stallion, which proved to be a superb animal; the captain afterward offered $800.00 for him.

We then retraced our steps slowly for a few miles, keeping a sharp lookout for the enemy, giving Joe an opportunity to overtake us, if such was his good fortune. I had seen Joe leap his horse over the fence and had taken in the lay of the land, so we reasoned that, barring accidents, he would join us soon. We left signals that none but our own party could read on the road telling him our route should he happen to see them. He soon overtook us laughing at the trick he had played on the "Johns."

14

Riding with the Rebels

Nor would I count among my friends,
My Country's enemy.

THE NEXT DAY, I think it was December 5th, we made a very early start
and got fifteen or eighteen miles to the right oblique by the time the sun
was an hour high. It was a frosty morning. We had got in a neighborhood
where we learned that the enemy had foraged the previous evening and
knew that they were present in some force not far away, but having some
important duty to attend to that day, we kept on. We soon came up with
a middle-aged and ragged Confederate soldier, mounted, who was either
out as a picket or foraging on his own account. He tried to play the citizen
dodge on us, saying that he lived in that neighborhood, but as he could
tell us the names of none of the inhabitants, we sized him up in his true
character. While we did not want to be bothered with prisoners, we thought
it safe to take him along rather than to leave him to scatter the news of our
presence in that vicinity. He could or would give us no information as to
the whereabouts of the enemy or the roads. He led us along an obscure road
through an old field grown up in pie bushes that prevented us from seeing
anything in our front. Suddenly we came plump into a main road that ran
at right angles to the course we were following. Just across this road and
close to it in a field, a regiment of Rebel cavalry had encamped the previous
night and were just then fallen in and were marching away to our left, the
direction we wished to go.

The rear of the column was yet in sight about forty rods away. As was
usual for the Confederate cavalry on such marches, there were a large
number of men remaining around the campfires, packing up and prepar-
ing to follow and overtake the main column. There must have been at least

twenty-five percent of the Rebel force thus straggling along, some in front of us, others in our rear, while still others not yet mounted but getting ready to do so. This was the most critical and sensational moment we had ever experienced. While many of them looked at us, no one appeared to pay any particular attention, supposing us to belong to their brigade or regiment. An alarm would have instantly brought a hundred guns to bear on us at short range. On reaching this main road, two of our boys were slightly in advance of the balance, and very wisely, without giving any sign of dismay, started to the left, following the course pursed by the enemy. Captain Duncan was riding just behind me and beside the prisoner, trying to pump him. I have always from boyhood prided myself on having great presence of mind in any sudden emergency. On this occasion one glance seemed to show me that our only chance lay in keeping up the deception and following the crowd until an opportunity presented itself for our escape.

There was danger, however, that our prisoner would give the alarm. Quick as thought, I stepped my horse aside and let Captain Duncan and the prisoner pass me, telling him in a low voice to keep right along and I would take care of the prisoner, at the same time pulling a revolver and resting it handily on my right knee. Just then the old man glanced at me and my gun, and when his eyes met mine, though not a word was spoken, I could see the tears roll down his cheeks. I remember quite distinctly what my thoughts were, that if no alarm was given, our chances for escape were largely in the majority, but on the other hand, if he should give the alarm, our only chance was to shoot him and strike for the woods. He seemed also to be of my mind and kept along beside the captain, occasionally looking back to me and my gun, but saying nothing. I could not help pitying the poor old fellow, he was certainly heartbroken, but we could not help it as self-preservation at that particular time was our first law.

Nothing could be more orderly than our march with the "Johns," with the enemy to the front of us, and enemy to the rear of us, besides many stragglers to the right of us. We preserved our distance and they theirs; that was all there was to it.

After the war, I met General Joe Wheeler in Savannah and related to him this incident. He said he had heard something about it at the time, and laughingly observed, "It was well for you, young man, that we did not catch you."

We marched in this manner perhaps half a mile, when I noticed a lane leading off to our left, to a house a couple of hundred yards from the main road, at which we could see a horse standing, without saddle or bridle. As Wheeler's men were ordered to pick up all horses of any service, the thought occurred to me that we might make this an excuse to part company with our friends, the enemy, so I called to those in front and suggested that we go up and look at that "hoss." Our advance being then at the entrance to the land, without more ado we started up to look at the "hoss." The rest followed their lead at a slow pace, the old man also, as we could not very well dispense with his company at that moment. As he turned into the lane, he again looked at me and I never saw a man of his age shed tears as he did. I reassured him somewhat by telling him that if he kept still, no harm would befall him. Captain Duncan afterward told us that he had told the old man that if he opened his mouth to give the alarm, that instant he would die, that his men were the most desperate men on earth and the old man believed him, and I don't blame him.

When we arrived opposite where the "hoss" was, which was on quite a rise of ground, we decided that we were not looking for any "hosses" and passed on over the hill, and when out of sight of "Mr. Wheeler's Critter Men," we put spurs to our horses and soon put a mile or two between us and them. Here we came to a halt and told our friend, the prisoner, that as he had proved himself a pretty good fellow and had given us no trouble, we would bid him an affectionate good-bye and he might return to his friends. If the reader can remember the time when he received his first pair of new red-top boots, or when he used to jump out of bed on a Christmas morning to see what Santa Claus had brought him, he can form some kind of an opinion of that old man when told he could go.

15

Canoe Expedition

And therefore will I strive my best for him
As for my father, and will go all lengths
To seek and find the murdered

ON THE FOLLOWING day, December 7th, Amick and I were ordered to cross the Ogeechee River and carry some dispatches across to the left wing, which duty took us the entire day. Returning and coming into a road a few miles behind the 17th Corps, we decided to overtake and camp with that corps that night. Just at sunset we came to a house occupied by poor people; near the road there stood a middle-aged woman and her grown, married daughter, who were screaming lustily. We approached them and inquired the cause when the old lady told us that two soldiers, stragglers from the main column, had, sometime after the army had passed, came to them and ravished the daughter, that they had been gone half an hour.[1]

General Howard had many times instructed the scouts to shoot such miscreants on sight, whenever found. This, however, was the only case of the kind we had heard of, and we proposed to follow on and overtake them, arrest and take them to General Sherman's headquarters. The old lady would not hear of our leaving them, however, saying that the men were now probably with their own command, so we could not find them or identify them, and urged us to remain and protect them till all danger was passed. We then found some corn for our horses but they could furnish us with nothing for our supper. However, we remained until they became somewhat quieted, when we departed.

I wish here to state that while history records that all large armies while marching through an enemy's country have been guilty to a greater or less extent of this heinous crime, Sherman's army can point with pride to the fact that so few of such infamous crimes were perpetrated, especially when it is considered that the army was so scattered over so large a territory and so many small detachments were foraging for the support of the army. This was the only case that came to our knowledge. There may have been others but we never heard of them. Further, it is safe to say that at least ninety percent of the army would have resented it by shooting down the perpetrator if caught.

The next morning, December 8th, we again crossed the Ogeechee River and joined the scouts who were just ready to go on an expedition to strike the Savannah and Florida Railroad to destroy communication of the Confederate Army at Savannah with the South. We arrived at the railroad some miles south of the river, but finding no bridges to burn, contented ourselves with cutting the telegraph wires. We had no tools of destruction aside from our weapons and it was amusing to see the boys try to shoot the wire in two. After several shots had been fired without success, I tried my hand by shooting at the glass insulator, which had the desired result at the first shot. After doing what damage we could, we returned to headquarters earlier than usual, having learned in the morning that another and more important expedition would demand our attention in the evening. Accordingly when we arrived at headquarters, which had been moved across to the north side of the river during the day, we found that Captain Duncan, who had not ridden with us that day, had secured a dugout canoe and some provisions and was ready to start down the river to communicate with the fleet, under Admiral Dahlgren, which was supposed to be awaiting the approach of Sherman's army at Ossabaw Sound. He selected Amick and myself to accompany him.[2] He carried dispatches from General Howard to Admiral Dahlgren, or whoever might prove to be in command of the fleet. I was probably selected because I had had some experience in handling canoes in the rivers of the lumber regions of Wisconsin. At any rate I was placed in the stern to manage the boat and steer, while the others also had a paddle each and assisted in propelling the now famous "ship."

The canoe was, as I now remember, about eighteen feet long and two feet wide. It had a round bottom and was evidently made by one who understood how a canoe should be built.

It was thought that we should be able to reach the fleet, if at all, in two nights' running, it not being considered safe to try to make headway in daylight. I cannot now remember if we had a map or chart of the river or sound, but if we did, it could be of no use to us in the nighttime, when we did not dare to strike a light.

16

Down the Ogeechee

By blows, by hardships, and all forms of ill.

ABOUT DARK WE bade good-bye to our friends and started for the sea. I will say here *en passant* that while we were looking for glory, this was an undertaking that we did not particularly fancy. Not being sailors and considering ourselves fairly good cavalrymen, we felt that we would much rather have been astride of a good horse than aboard the best ship in the fleet. However, we were in for it and away we went.

The night was a clear starlight one, just light enough for us to see to keep our course and not run into obstructions. It was also light enough so that any pickets stationed along the bank could have seen us if in the middle of the stream. As a rule, the banks were eight to twelve feet above the water, so that by keeping close to the bank, we could not be seen by any of the enemy's pickets unless they should be on the brink and looking down at us. Of course, we could not be seen from the opposite side because we would be in the shadows and the bank would act as a dark background. Our speed was necessarily slow on account of having to proceed without noise. The night was cold for that climate and we soon came in sight of the reflection of camp or picket fires, which in many instances would be but a few feet from us but hidden from our sight by the high banks. We made good headway considering our difficulties, but as we did not dare to speak above a whisper, it seemed the longest night we ever experienced. Just before daybreak we passed King's Bridge, close to the bank.[1] It was well for us that we were under cover, for we could not see the bridge until we got nearly to it. We could hear voices directly over us on the bridge, conversing in a low tone. We would like to have halted there to hear what they were saying but could not stop our speed without causing a disturbance in the water. Besides, about this time our hearts had risen and were located somewhere about our thorax, and were thumping a tattoo that alarmed us, for fear the Reb pickets would hear it. The river, so far, had been very straight and swift, but now that we passed the first great danger, the bridge, we found the river widening out and becoming very crooked. We saw no more picket fires that night and succeeded in getting down to within a couple of miles of Fort McAllister, where, daylight overtaking us, we pulled into a bunch of willows near a plantation house, where we concealed our dugout and awaited developments.[2]

It seemed that a road ran down from King's Bridge to Fort McAllister on the right side of the river. At the point where we were, the road to the plantation house was located off the river a hundred or more yards. The negro quarters were between the river and road. After maneuvering around for a while, we succeeded in decoying an old negro to our place of concealment, who, on being told who we were and our mission, advised us to remain where we were till night. He said their master, or overseer, kept a strict watch on the quarters and that it would be unsafe for us to venture out. He also said that the hands on this plantation were kept on such short allowance of rations that they could not supply us with any. He, however, brought us some water and agreed to keep watch for us through the day; he, being a very old man, was not required to work in the fields but only to do odd jobs, or as we Yankees call it, "chores," around the plantation yards.

This old man could give us no information whatever that would be of value to us, but stated that we ought not to attempt to run by the obstructions at the fort until after midnight. He also told us that at about dark we could drop down the river about a mile to the McAllister plantation, where we would be able to get some provisions and more reliable information.

We got some sleep through the day, and when night came on and it was sufficiently dark, we resumed our journey and arrived at the McAllister plantation in due time, where we found a first-class plantation, everything up in trim, the quarters being located in a fine ark of live oaks and but a few rods from the river. We soon found some fairly intelligent negroes, who prepared us a good supper, and one sprightly young negro who was a servant for his master at the fort directed us how to pass the fort in safety. He stated that at the mouth of the river and opposite the fort, there was a row of piles driven across the river about twenty feet apart, and connected together by a chain, and that there were torpedoes placed occasionally along between the piles.[3] He further said that we had better not start till quite late, and even after we got through the obstructions, we should keep a sharp lookout for Rebel pickets, who were stationed in a boat below keeping watch for deserters, who were occasionally deserting to our blockading vessel outside. He also said that there was a strong Rebel picket post at the opposite side of the river at the end of the row of piles. He could not tell us much about the blockading vessel outside—where it was located, nor anything concerning it that would aid us in finding it. As was customary with us, we had stationed young negroes on the outside of the house to give us warning of the approach of white people.

We had just finished our supper when an alarm was given that there were Rebel soldiers from the fort near the door. We all skipped out the back door, each going his own way. Amick gained a bunch of holly bushes and hid among the thorns. I do not know where Duncan was concealed, but we always accused him of squatting down in a corner and getting an old fat negro mammy to sit on him. I crowded under the house, which was built up off the ground nearly three feet. The house was soon surrounded on every side by perhaps twenty mounted soldiers. I could see their horses' feet on all sides not over ten feet from me. They remained perhaps ten minutes and then departed. The negroes informed us that this was a regular patrol that made nightly visits among the negro quarters and along the roads to see that negroes were all at their homes. We had feared that they had got an inkling of our presence, but on this as well as on all other occasions, the negroes were true to us. I will except one time when I was betrayed by a negro, and I am now of the opinion that he did so because he thought I was a Reb in disguise.

After the patrol was gone, we came out and the young negro servant told us that this visit was something unusual and he feared they had learned somehow of our presence in the neighborhood and advised us to get away as soon as possible, which we lost no time in doing.

We were now in tide water and the tide was against us, so we crossed over to the other side and, keeping close to the bank, floated slowly down towards the dreaded obstructions.

About ten or eleven o'clock, the tide turned and we made a little better time and finally came to the piling, where we passed between the shore pile and the bank, which were about thirty feet apart. Just above us on the bank, we could see the reflection of a bright light not many feet distant and could hear two or three men talking, but we were not noticed and soon passed out of view. We could see the lights at the fort across the river and hear the sentries walking their beats.

17

Rescued in the Bay

And lo! The ocean billows murmured loud.

AT THIS POINT the bay widened out to a mile in width, and a little farther down the sound, it was two or three miles wide, with a broad opening to the sea. A night breeze had sprung up from the sea and soon the water become so rough that we were in danger of being capsized. We then kept close to the left bank so that in case of accident we could gain the shore. We here found that the high banks had disappeared and in their place was a low salt marsh which overflowed at every high tide. We succeeded in getting two or three miles down the bay, when it became so rough that we pulled our dugout up on the marsh among the salt grass and lay down in it and went to sleep.

The next morning about the first "peep-o-day," I was awakened by feeling the boat rock under me, and looking up, I discovered that the returning tide had set us afloat in two feet of water. None of us were accustomed to tides, hence were not looking out for this experience. It was now light enough for us to see that there was an island in the sound that shut us off from view of the sea. We at this time thought this island was a part of the mainland and decided that our best plan was to cross to it and coast along till we could get a glimpse of the blockading vessel—besides we were yet in sight of the fort, from which we could be seen as soon as it got light enough. We then paddled across to the island, where we landed and found the ruins of an ancient plantation house made of grout.[1] The fields had grown up in good-sized trees, one of which I climbed to see if I could get a sight of the ship. The other trees obstructed my view so that we could not see enough to get our bearings. We at first thought of waiting here for a while, but reflecting that the army was anxious to open up communications with the fleet at *the earliest possible* moment, we decided to try another plan. A land breeze had spring up which was favorable to our movements, as was also the outgoing tide. We took a diagonal course for the opposite shore, about two miles distant, and had proceeded but about halfway, when the open sea showed up on our right and we saw the blockading ship loom up, about six miles distant off the bar and about four miles from extreme point of land.

Here was our haven, the sight of which made our hearts glad. However, we also saw at a glance that our troubles were not over, for there was between us and the ship a heavy sea running. We paddled our way slowly toward the ship for some time, but did not notice, in our anxiety, that the wind and tide were carrying us rapidly out to sea, the wind being on our right rear quarter. We were rapidly drifting in a direction that would leave the ship two or more miles to our right. We were now advanced so far that we could not retreat even if we had wanted to. The sea by this time was very rough and our boat was so small and frail that we were compelled to keep her headed across the waves to keep from capsizing.

To make matters worse, we then discovered a boat and boat's crew on the beach on the island to our right, near to the land's end and about parallel to us. We saw them hastily embark and hoist a sail and steer toward us. The wind favored them and they came rapidly and we saw that we were in for trouble. We had been keeping a sharp lookout for the Rebel picket boat the negro had spoken of, and here it was heaving down on us, and we in a small dugout, in the rough seas, having all we could do to keep afloat.

We saw at a glance that there was nothing for us to do but to quietly submit to capture and for a few minutes did nothing but speculate as to the reception we would receive at the hands of our captors.

Amick offered the suggestion that we could not claim to be Rebel deserters, and being in disguise in the enemy's lines, we would be held as spies and shot at sunrise next morning. In the midst of these speculations, the boat had approached to within hailing distance and they hailed us "Boat ahoy!" We answered the hail and were summoned to "Heave to!" and at the same moment we saw the eight men in the boat as if by one motion, raise eight muskets. When Captain Duncan asked, and I shall always remember it the longest day I live, "Quimby, you have many times helped us out of bad scrapes, tell us how to get out of this?"

Now, I want to go back a little in my story and say, that when I first joined the scout corps, the most of the scouts being of longer experience, and I being a stranger to all, they, as I thought, looked upon me as a new recruit is always looked upon by old soldiers, that is, as a "greeny," a "Tenderfoot." This made a deep impression on me and I always felt that there was something to learn that I had not been taught, and that the others had learned. When Captain Duncan asked that question, I felt like a boy who has just learned that he is a man. That I was rated as high as or higher than any of them made me feel as though I could attack many times our number without fear. I want to say also that up to that moment I had not conceived any plan by which we could extricate ourselves from the terrible fix we were in, but in the twinkling of an eye, a plan did occur to me, and I said, "If you both will do as I say, I think we can save ourselves or at least part of us." I said, "Let us each get out both pistols and lay them where they can be quickly reached, then pretend to surrender, and when they (the enemy) draw near us and are off their guard, seize the guns and kill every one of them, take their boat, and gain the ship." Both agreed to the plan and we got the revolvers ready and awaited the enemy's approach with palpitating hearts. Then much to our surprise and gratification, we saw the man at the helm reach down and take up a small flag and set it in the stern, which unfolded to our view the beautiful American emblem of Liberty. In our excitement we had failed to notice that the men were dressed in navy blue.[2]

Ever since that moment, I have been able to comprehend the emotions felt by shipwrecked sailors who have been afloat for days in unknown seas, without food, water, or compass, on beholding relief at hand. These men proved to be sailors of the blockading ship and had made their daily trip to the shore to gather oysters for the use of the ship's crew. They had seen us by the aid of a glass before we had observed them and supposed us to be a party of Rebel deserters who were trying to make the ship, had pursued us merely as an act of mercy, knowing that in our small boat and by reason of the rough seas just outside, we would never be able to reach the ship, but would certainly perish.

Our rescuers told us that Admiral Dahlgren had ordered blockading ships along the coast to keep a sharp lookout for any messenger that General Sherman might send out. Knowing that the Federal forces held no points of land from Charleston to Florida, the only means of communication would be by the plan actually adopted.

Our rescuers took us in their boat, took our dugout in tow, and returned to the beach from which they had just come, and after pulling the dugout well up on the beach, took us on board the ship. I am unable to give the name of this blockading vessel at the present time, but have a faint recollection that it was something like, "Bellerophon." As I before stated, I kept no diary or notes and have had to depend upon history for dates and names to a great extent. However, I think that the reader will agree with me, when I say that, after thirty-seven years, in recording these events my memory has treated me fairly well.[3]

18

General Howard's Version

He by my side may stand, and witness bear.

In an article by General O. O. Howard, published in the *National Tribune* of January 23, 1896, referring to this expedition, he says:

> Just before this operation of investment commenced, - the 9th day of December, after our last combat and near the Savannah Canal, I drew up a dispatch to the Commander of the Naval forces to this effect:
>
> Sir: We have met with perfect success thus far. Troops in fine spirits and near by.
> Respectfully,
> O.O. Howard,
> Major-General Commanding

I have always been under the impression that I inserted "Sherman" before "near by," but the above is the form in with the dispatch has always appeared.

Captain William Duncan was to take with him Sergeant Myron J. Amick and Sergeant George W. Quimby and proceed down the Ogeechee, passing Confederate Stations, the King's Bridge, Fort McAllister and all obstructions and go out to sea and communicate with the fleet. It seemed next to impossible that the feat could be accomplished, but Capt. Duncan's already distinguished career as a scout and his confidence that he could accomplish the enterprise, led me to try. He secured a long dugout rather narrow and somewhat weather worn; then putting into it such rations as he thought he would require, he took this dispatch and another one from my signal officer, and set out. He went along very well by night, having passed the bridge and carefully worked through the torpedo obstructions.

When the day dawned the morning of the 10th, he found some negroes who befriended him and his men. The party kept pretty well under cover until evening. During the night the party appears to have made considerable progress, but did not succeed in getting past Fort McAllister. They went ashore to get a guide and some provisions, if it were possible among the blacks, their boat was tied up and then they worked their way through some bushes and thin groves till they came near a roadway. Here, they heard voices of some Confederates passing along the road. By lying down and keeping quiet, they were not discovered. Soon after this they came to quite a sizable negro house, went in and were well treated and were refreshed with provisions. While they were eating they heard a party of cavalry riding toward the house. The negroes quickly concealed them under the floors; the houses there generally without cellars, can be so conveniently used. The coolness and smartness of the negroes surprised even Capt. Duncan who believed in them and trusted them. Very soon after their visitors had gone the negroes guided them back to their boat.

In such operations as these with hairbreadth escapes, they hid through the 11th in the daytime. When night came to avoid one danger they crossed the wide river; but hearing some voices they feared a recapture from that bank, so they quietly pushed away avoiding a boat filled with oarsmen that was passing over the Ogeechee from a Confederate gun-boat at anchor below Fort McAllister. They ran so near this gun-boat that they were in terror for fear that some noise that they had to make in paddling or a flash-light from the vessel, would discover them; but surprising to say they had passed all obstacles and soon after daylight on the morning of the 12th they drifted out in the broad bay.

There the *Dandelion*, a dispatch boat of the Navy discovered the dugout with its three weary scouts, joyful enough to be thus found. They were taken on board and carried to Port Royal Harbor, to the Flag Steamer *Philadelphia*, arriving about eight o'clock the same morning. I can imagine Duncan's satisfaction when he saw my brief dispatch put into the hands of Rear-Admiral Dahlgren, to whom it was addressed.

I have never seen Admiral Dahlgren's report of it published, so I extract a few words from it; "perhaps no event could give greater satisfaction to the country than that which I announce and I beg leave to congratulate the United States Government on its occurrence.

It may perhaps be exceeding my province, but as I cannot refrain from expressing the hope that the Department will commend Captain Duncan and his companions to the Honorable Secretary of War for some mark of approbation for the success in establishing communication between General Sherman and the fleet. It was an enterprise that required both skill and courage."

As hereafter explained, General Howard was in error as to the *Dandelion*. We did not see that boat until 4 o'clock P.M. of that day, when it was on its return from Florida.

Nearly all the newspapers of the North published their versions of the story of our experience, none of which came within "gunshot" of the facts.

Except in a few minor details, where my memory may have failed me, this narrative is true in every particular.

General Sherman and General Howard have both stated in their description of this event that the dispatch boat *Dandelion* had picked us up. This is an error, as we did not see the *Dandelion* for five or six hours after we reached the ship.

This day, if I remember correctly, was on a Thursday,[1] and it was the regular day on which the dispatch boat *Dandelion* made her weekly trip from Hilton Head to the Aetamaha River to deliver dispatches, the mail, and fresh food to the different blockading vessels stationed along the coast. She had passed down early in the morning and would not return till towards evening. She did return about 4 P.M. and took us aboard and started post haste for Hilton Head, where Admiral Dahlgren and the fleet were stationed. We did not reach Hilton Head till the next morning. I think about or a little after sunrise, and steamed directly for the flag-ship, where we delivered the dispatches to Admiral Dahlgren. I have always been of the opinion that the flag-ship was the *Philadelphia*, but General Sherman in his memoirs states it was the *Silver Moon*.[2] I cannot account for this discrepancy. It may be that we were both correct, as it is possible, and I think probably, that the flag-ship was the *Philadelphia*, but that by reason of its greater draft of water, he may have transferred his flag to that of the *Silver Moon*, a ship of lighter draft, to enable him to navigate more shallow waters. However, this may be another case where my memory is at fault.

19

On the Flag-Ship

THERE WERE MANY hundreds of ships of all descriptions anchored in the harbor of Port Royal.

Soon after the admiral had read the dispatches, signals were made by flags and soon much excitement seemed to prevail, as ship boats could be seen darting in all directions, in every part of the harbor and to and from the shore.

It is not, perhaps, within my province to make criticism of my superior officers and those of much greater age and experience, but I cannot resist the temptation to offer the following thoughts that were presented to mind at the time, and I presume they occurred to many another unsophisticated "Country Jake."

The veterans of sixty-three, -four, and -five will remember how at times, when Colonel Slow or General Easy would be ordered to make a quick movement on the enemy, or to gain some advantageous position, they would commence, to prepare, to get ready, to obey the order—then they would prepare, then get ready, then start, and finally after hours or days of procrastination, they would be too late, too late. This slowness on the part of some officers probably cost more unnecessary sacrifice of life than all other causes during the war. This did not apply to such officers as Hancock, Sheridan, Logan, McPherson, Howard, and host of others, who always executed an order *at once*, and their superior officers could always count on them in every emergency. On the other hand, there were many others, who although good and patriotic men at heart, were so constituted that they could not act with promptness, or as the saying is now, "get a move on themselves."

Young as I was at the time, I can remember that I became impatient at the slow movements of the navy in response to the invitation of General Sherman for them to cooperate in the opening of communications with the outer world, and the reduction of Fort McAllister. It seemed to my inexperienced mind at the time, that being ready as they were always supposed to be, the order should have been given within fifteen minutes of our arrival to weigh anchor and "fly to the rescue" under full steam and sail, instead of a delay of two days as was the case.

I suppose, however, that I was in the wrong, but I cannot help making these reflections. This, however, I am certain of, that I would not have wanted one of those "conservative" commanders as a comrade while scouting.

We were taken in charge by the officers of the Ward Room of the flag-ship, where we were wined and dined and questioned until we were nearly exhausted. The officers of the navy were a lot of gentlemanly fellows who spared no pains to entertain us to the best of their ability, and I want to say that their ability far exceeded that of the line officers of the army in time of war.

Among other things, I remember that they were very anxious and even persistent in securing from us everything we possessed as mementos, even our coats, hats, shoes, revolvers, pocket knives, and pocketbooks, were asked for. They offered us more than four times their value in money besides furnishing us with their equivalent in navy clothing, weapons, etc. Of course, we declined the money part of the transaction. They complained that they had been tied up during the most of the war in doing blockade duty, and had had no opportunity of gaining glory or securing mementos. They assured us that they intended sending our dugout to Boston, but I have never learned if it was done.

We remained on board the flag-ship that day and night. The next morning Captain Duncan and Amick learned that they had some acquaintances in an Illinois Regiment on shore at Hilton Head and asked to be set on shore to visit them. I, having no such acquaintances on shore there, concluded to remain aboard. Soon after their departure, the fleet inspecting officer informed me that he was going at once on a tour of inspection through all the war vessels in the Harbor and invited me to accompany him, which invitation I gladly accepted. I do not remember anything in particular that attracted my attention except the visit to the old "three decker" and the *Pawnee*. The magnitude and appointments of this old time battleship made me stare to "beat the band." We returned to the flag-ship sometime in the afternoon and Admiral Dahlgren immediately sent for me. He notified me that he was extremely anxious to send a dispatch to General Sherman and asked me if I thought I could deliver it. He stated that it would be too late to send on shore for Duncan and Amick. I answered him that I thought it possible, provided I had a good man to go with me. He asked me then if I thought I could make shift with a sailor as a companion.

I had become acquainted with a bright young midshipman whose name I have now forgotten, who had expressed to me his dissatisfaction of the close confinement of life on board of a ship, and on learning that I would be permitted to make my own selection of a comrade, urged me to name him as the one desired. I did so, but the admiral refused to permit an officer to leave without first having tendered his resignation. The midshipman immediately wrote out his resignation, which he accepted.

The admiral then gave us an order on the proper officer for anything we might need for our trip. We thus secured a new suit of navy officer's uniform, without insignia, and each a pair of fine navy revolvers, besides all the rations we could consent to carry. I had told the admiral that I wanted to be put ashore on the north shore of Ossabaw Sound, at night, as close up to Fort McAllister as we could get without attracting the attention of the enemy. Soon the dispatch was ready and the admiral gave to me an order for Captain Williamson of the dispatch boat *Dandelion*, to land us at any point on Ossabaw Sound that we may suggest. "Give them every facility."

20

Fort McAllister Falls

And loud and fierce their battle clan,
Like screams of angry Vultures rang.

WE ARRIVED IN the sound about twelve o'clock the next day. I requested
Captain Williamson to delay his approach to the upper end of the sound
till dark. He explained to me, however, that it was a weekly occurrence for
a gunboat to go up and exchange a few shots with Fort McAllister and then
retire, that the motive of our approach would not be properly construed
by the enemy. He in turn suggested that we go up slowly toward the fort
and that about sunset he would put me in a small boat, properly manned,
which would be concealed behind the gunboat and at the proper point we
could cut loose and gain the shore, that the boat's crew after landing us
could overtake the ship, then he could go up farther and throw a shot or
two at the fort to attract their attention, thus enabling us to get as far as
possible toward dry ground before darkness overtook us. It was well that
matters turned out differently than the way I had planned, as I afterward
learned that we would not have been able to reach the army by reason of the
intervention of several bayous or salt water creeks that would have cut us off
from the mainland.

However, the boat was got in readiness and we were about to embark
when an officer on deck who had been watching with a glass suddenly
caught sight of a flag on the land northwest of the fort, which appeared to
be signaling.

Immediately the signal officer came forward with his code and flag and
signaled, "Who are you?" but could not read the answer. From my description of the probable situation of the army, it could not be other than Sherman's army. He then discovered that he had got the wrong code, and that

the new code which had been recently introduced in the army, copies of which had been furnished to the navy, was the one to be used. He then hastily ran down the companionway and fished out the new code, and repeated the question, when he was at once answered, "General Sherman." He then asked, "Is the fort taken?" but did not receive an answer for some time. They appeared to be very busy signaling someone in another direction, whom we could not see.

Almost immediately, the sound of heavy cannonading could be heard by us from the direction of the fort, which was soon followed by volleys of musketry and loud cheering, then all was still.

We rightly concluded that the fort was being attacked, but with what result we could not guess. Then our flag repeated the question "Is the fort taken?" and was immediately answered, "Yes." It was now no longer necessary for us scouts to proceed by land as we could proceed much quicker and easier by water.

On account of torpedoes which were supposed to be planted in the water near the fort, it was thought best to be very careful not to run afoul of one of them, so we steamed up slowly a little farther till we could see the fort more plainly.

Right here I must differ from the statement made by General Sherman in his *Memoirs* in which he states that it was in the night that he came aboard the *Dandelion*.[1] My recollection tells me that it was about twilight. That Captain Williamson was about to send us ashore with our dispatches when a boat was seen approaching us from the shore. He further says that "General Howard accompanied him." Now I have no recollection of General Howard coming aboard at that time, but General Howard has since informed me that General Sherman is correct. I remember him and two or three other officers coming aboard, and after shaking hands with the officers of the gunboat and exchanging a few remarks, I stepped forward and handed the dispatches from Admiral Dalhgren, together with a late New York *Herald* which contained accounts of the Battle of Franklin. The general, after hastily reading the dispatches, turned to the *Herald* and read aloud the particulars of the battle and appeared to be much more interested in that subject than in his own affairs.

The only way I can explain this difference of recollection of General Sherman and myself is that he was so busily engaged in so many matters that he has two different visits to the gunboat mixed in his mind and has referred to his later one or has confused the two. If there are any members of the crew of the *Dandelion* who shall read this, I think they will be able to corroborate me in my statement. However, the discrepancy is immaterial.

General Sherman in his *Memoirs*, Volume II, page 197, says:

> At that very moment some one discovered a faint cloud of smoke, and an object gliding as it were, along the horizon above the tops of the sedge toward the sea, which little by little grew till it was pronounced to be the smokestack of a steamer coming up the river. "It must be one of our squadron." Soon the flag of the United States was plainly visible, and our attention was divided between the approaching steamer and the expected assault. When the sun was about an hour high, another signal message came from General Hazen, that he was ready and I replied to go ahead, as a friendly steamer was approaching from below. Soon we made out a group of officers of the deck of this vessel, signaling with a flag, "Who are you?" The answer went back promptly, "General Sherman." Then followed the question, "Is the Fort taken?"

On the next page (198), he says, "The good news [was] instantly sent by signal officer to our navy friends on the approaching gunboat, for a point of timber had shut out Fort McAllister from their view and they had not seen the action at all, but must have heard the cannonading."

I am confident that General Sherman is again mistaken, as my recollection is that while signaling him, we were in sight of the fort, but being two or three miles away and low down on the deck of a tugboat, we could not determine the true situation, hence the question, "Is the Fort taken?"

We remained on board of the *Dandelion* that night, and next morning went ashore on the north side of the river. I had a great curiosity to see just how close we had been to the enemy's pickets on the night we passed the obstructions, and from the appearance of their campfires and the path made by the sentry, while walking his beat, we could not have been farther from him than thirty-five or forty feet. We can attribute our good fortune in passing him unnoticed to the fact that it being a cold night, he may have been over at the fire warming his fingers.

We then walked up to the rice plantation of Mr. Cheever[2] that had been used by General Sherman the previous day as a signal station, where we found two of our scouts who piloted us to our headquarters, where I spent the balance of the day in describing our trip as "water cavalrymen."

We learned from them that two days after our departure, they had had a very hard scrap with a squadron of Rebel cavalry. It seems that the boys had got the "Johns" in somewhat of a box, and stampeded them down a lane, and taking advantage of the panic had, by reason of having better horses, run them down and captured thirty-two of them with their horses and arms.

I have often since read accounts of this expedition, written by sensational writers, not one of which came within "a mile" of the truth. If one was to believe their story, he would almost believe that we had captured or killed Rebels by the score and sunk gunboats galore, but the actual facts were as I have given them, as near as I can now remember.

The reader will remember that during the war, the local newspapers were in the habit of eulogizing the soldiers of their own state who had become conspicuous by valorous deed, oftentimes to the discredit of soldiers of other states who were equally entitled to praise. It was so in my state (Wisconsin). My name was heralded by them as the only great scout, etc., etc., when as a matter of fact, there were several others of other states who were equally, if not more, entitled to fame than I was.

It was said that there were dozens of men after the war, of the "Si Kleg" order, who boasted that they had scouted with "Quimby." I remember one of them was telling his exploits when scouting with "Quimby"; when I asked him for particulars of some of the events referred to, he readily related them. You can imagine his crestfallen looks when I told him that I was "Quimby."

21

Siege of Savannah

DURING THE SIEGE of Savannah, the scouts had very little duty to perform, as Kilpatrick's cavalry were across the river to range the country and protect the right flank, while the left wing was resting on the Savannah River and needing no scouts.

We, as individuals, spent most of the time in visiting our friends along the line of investment. Captain Duncan and Amick returned to us in a couple of days, having come in one of the transports of the fleet which had now arrived and was in the lower bay awaiting the removal of the obstructions in the river.

I rode down to King's Bridge and the Cheever plantation the next day, where I found the obstructions removed and the river full of transports, and there were acres of army supplies being unloaded, and the "Cracker" line was opened.[1]

While the army was settling down around Savannah, I had occasion to go some distance to visit some of friends in a Wisconsin Regiment. I overtook General Osterhaus, his staff, and body guard. Of course, discipline and military etiquette would not allow me to ride on past them, so I lingered in their rear. The woods at this time were full of crows and General Osterhaus was having considerable fun, boasting of his marksmanship. One of his aides challenged him to fire at one of the crows, on the wager of a bottle of wine. The general fired and missed. Another wager was made and he fired, and while the crow flew away, he claimed that he had wounded it. Part of the staff supported his claim and the balance took sides against him. They finally rode on, having much amusement over the affair. I, then, waited till they had passed on and the crows had become quieted, then dismounted and, taking careful aim, fired and was fortunate enough to kill one of them. I picked him up and, mounting, soon overtook the cavalcade, rode up to the general, and saluting, handed him the crow, saying: "General, here is the crow you shot." The tables were turned on the opposition and a great uproar followed. I think the general never enjoyed a small joke more than that one.

As I rode away, one of the opposition called to me, "Say, Mr. Scout, shoot one for me, too," but the general would not have it that way, but insisted that it was his game.

After the settling down of the army to the siege of Savannah, and before the arrival of supplies from the fleet, the men were becoming hard pressed for the necessaries of life. There was some meat on hand but little or no hard bread or meal. It is true there was a plentiful supply of rice, but this was in the husk. This husk is as difficult to remove as the husk of oats. The men soon learned from the negroes that it could be removed only by pounding in a mortar. Soon every company was provided with an improvised mortar, made from a log of wood, and a club for a pestle. One passing along the lines could see thousand of these "rice mills" in operation at all times, day or night.

This rice filled a long-felt want, and much amusement was furnished in chaffing the luckless soldiers who had to do the pounding.

During the siege of Savannah, I went with the scouts one day some distance south of the Ogeechee River on no business in particular but in general to see that the enemy were not prowling around our right and rear. On this trip we came to a plantation which was devoted largely to the raising of sugar cane. We found about a dozen barrels of fairly good brown sugar, one of which we confiscated and took to the camp for the use of the scouts. When it is considered that while many other kinds of rations were plentiful with us, and that sugar was generally issued to us in spoonfuls, it will be seen at once that this was a great acquisition to our larder.

The soldiers of the army, and more particularly of the Western Army, were prone to pick up or manufacture new words or expressions. When a new word became popular, it would soon become of common use throughout that portion of the army. The word "shebang" was early used by east and west, north and south, to mean a building used for any purpose of a public nature, either reputable or disreputable, from a sutler's shop to a hotel.

"Skedaddle" was another one that soon became universally used to take the place of all, run, skip, retreat, escape, etc., etc. A new word or an old one with a new and novel application would be taken up by the boys and soon it would be in universal use.

I remember an instance where the scouts were caught in a long lane or fenced road, with a large force of the enemy in front and rear. We were compelled to open the fence and make for the woods and were quickly followed by the enemy, who tried to surround us and effect our capture. We were at length stampeded and compelled to scatter and everyone strike out for himself. The first one who arrived in camp reported the balance all killed or captured. Later another came and reported that he had succeeded in making his escape but that the balance were overwhelmed. Still later another and still another came in with the same story. When the last one except myself came in, he reported that he had seen two Confederates ride me down, that I had shot and killed one but that the other had cut me down with his saber. While they were mourning over my loss, etc., I rode in upon them, and the one who had reported my death began inquiring how I had succeeded in getting away. He asked, "Did I not see two Rebs ride down upon you, etc.?" I answered, "Yes." He then asked, "Well, didn't I see you shoot one of them and the other bear down on you with uplifted saber?" I told him he probably did. "Then," he asked, "how did you manage to escape?" I told him that I pulled down on the 'John' and he . . ." I wanted to say "skedaddled," but for the life of me I could not think of the word, so I said "fled." Now the word "fled" was proper enough and quite applicable in this case, but was scarcely ever used except in books, and it struck all my hearers as being comical and a general laugh followed. The word afterward became of common use among the scouts in place of "skedaddle."

The funny part of it was that the man who had reported my death seemed hurt because he had been caught spreading a false report.

22

In Savannah

Nor let them banish from their city fear;
For who 'mong men, uncurbed by fear, is just.

As soon as the enemy evacuated Savannah, which was during the night of December 20th,[1] we moved with General Howard's headquarters into the city, where we took possession of an unoccupied two-story residence near the Pulaski monument, where we remained nearly four weeks and enjoyed ourselves with banquets, card playing, horse racing, etc. At one of these races, Jerry Phelan, who still had his high-jumping mare, was giving some exhibitions of his horse's qualifications, when he received a fall that broke his leg, shoulder, and several ribs. He was then sent to a hospital and I never saw him again. I have learned that several years since, he was drowned in an accident near Peoria, Illinois.

As soon as I could find the time, I made inquires for Captain Stevenson and learned that he was still living at his South Carolina home, and that by reason of an old injury, was now unable to leave his chair or bed without assistance. His daughter, Miss Mollie, had recently come into the city and reported that a portion of General Wheeler's cavalry had taken all their provisions and their last cow, leaving them destitute, together with all their neighbors. That she had purchased a small supply of provisions and left on the last train on the Charleston railroad that left the city, and that as the road was cut and the bridge across the Savannah River destroyed within two hours after the train's departure, they were unable to say whether or not she had arrived safely at home.

On showing my letter of introduction to these friends, they informed me just where and how I should find the family if I ever chanced in that vicinity.

After we had become comfortably settled in our quarters in the city, we went to General Sherman's office to draw our extra pay as scouts. As before stated, we were paid from a fund called "The Secret Service Fund." This fund, as I have been informed, was raised by the sale of confiscated and condemned property. The money was first paid over to the Secretary of War, or to someone designated by him to receive it, and by him turned over or parceled out to the various army commanders to be used by them as their judgment might dictate, without being required to account for its expenditure.

He gave all of us our regular $5.00 per day, but when he came to pay Amick and me the extra money for carrying the dispatches to the fleet, he only gave each of us $100.00. I protested at this and said to him, "General, you paid the man you sent to Knoxville with a dispatch for General Burnside $500.00, and it was not half as hazardous a trip as was this one to the ships." The general said. "Yes, I know it, boys, but you must remember that the government is very hard up now, and I have not got the money. I'll tell you what I can do. I'll give you the next chance that I may have, when I probably will have more money on hand with which to pay you." I said, "Very well, General, if you will do that, I will be satisfied." And so the matter rested.

As an illustration of the criminal acts of robbery that occurred on the march to the sea, I wish to give here an incident that came under my personal observation.

A villainous-looking negro who had probably been a hanger-on or camp follower took up his lodgings with our servants. While at Savannah and as provisions were plentiful with us, we made no objections, until one day my own servant came to me and related that this strange negro was a thief and was continually quarreling with our blacks and that he had attempted to carve up one of them with a razor. I went to the kitchen and belabored the villain with the flat of a saber and drove him off the premises. On searching his plunder, I found one hundred and seven razors that he had probably stolen from the citizens along the March. Razors seem to have been a mania with him, as no other plunder was found.

Another incident that came under my notice at Savannah was when one Arnold S. Tabor, a quartermaster sergeant at 17th Corps headquarters, quartered in the city, gave a banquet at which Amick and myself were invited. There were about fifteen invited guests present, all of whom partook freely of the good things of life, among which was a good assortment of viands, and all joined in voting the host and banquet a decided success. This banquet was held in a part of a large building in which a large amount of confiscated goods was stored, under the care and charge of Sergeant Tabor. We learned later that during our "Carnival" that night, that forty barrels of whiskey were stolen from the goods stored and that they were never recovered.

A year or two later, I learned that Tabor, after his discharge on arriving at home, drew $60,000 from his home bank and next morning left the city with his family, and has never since been heard of by his acquaintances.

When I consider that he had no bank account at the time of his enlistment, I have concluded that the banquet was given so that the guests could be witnessed that he had taken no part in the purloining of the liquor, and that this and other similar peccadilloes accounted for the swelling of his bank account.

23

The Stevensons

ABOUT JANUARY 15, 1865, the scouts accompanying General Howard's headquarters took passage for Beaufort, South Carolina. Immediately on arriving at Beaufort, the army advanced on Pocateligo [Pocotaligo] on the Charleston and Savannah railroad, which point General Foster's men had repeatedly tried to occupy without success.[1]

There was a good road leading to that place, but a part of the way several salt water sloughs intervened over which high grades and bridges had been built. A small force of the enemy resisted our advance at one of those bridges. The advance was delayed here until General Howard in person came up. On either side of this road a row of trees had grown up which obstructed the view, and General Howard, noticing Amick and I near at hand, handed his glass to us and sent us to our left to an old field to see the situation if possible. When we arrived at the point mentioned, we found a dense growth of weeds of perhaps eight feet high, which prevented our getting a good view. We then halted and stood up on our horses to better see the enemy. We had been in this position not to exceed two minutes when a Rebel eight-pound cannon, which was located across one of the salt marshes, about four hundred yards distant, turned loose on us at point-blank range. They had evidently taken us for a group of officers, perhaps a general and his staff. The shell exploded between us at perhaps twenty feet above our heads, but fortunately neither of us nor our horses were hit. I need not add that by the time they had reloaded their piece, we had found a more favorable location.

General Blair had by that time succeeded in effecting a crossing at another point and, swinging around, captured a portion of the Rebs, who on learning that ours was a part of Sherman's army, said that if they had known that "Old Billy" had got around there, they would have skipped at once.

This corps soon occupied Pocateligo, where they were soon joined by the 15th Corps, where they settled down to make preparations for the great march through the Carolinas.

Headquarters and the scouts returned to Beaufort. The scout corps was disbanded and immediately reorganized with the following named men: Lieutenant John McQueen, Chief of Scouts; M. J. Amick; George W. Quimby; Joe A. Bedoll; Bob Collins; Pat Wallace; John A. White; and Job Dawson. Two others whose names I have forgotten were also detailed, on the recommendation of some high officer, but they soon proved to be entirely worthless as scouts and only good for plundering citizens' houses and were returned to their commands to carry a gun and knapsack the balance of the campaign.

While lying at Beaufort, and the scouts having nothing of importance to do, I got permission from General Howard to be absent for a few days—and he, after being informed of the object of furlough, bid me "God Speed."

I had made inquiries at Beaufort and learned that a good road led to the Broad River, a distance of ten miles, where by crossing the river, four miles wide there (it being rather a bay or estuary), to Boyd's Landing. A good road then led to Grahamville, S.C., via of, and within two miles of, the celebrated battlefield of Honey Hill, where General Foster, commanding the Federal forces, got unmercifully thrashed by a much inferior force, and they, militia and home guards at that.[2]

On arriving at Boyd's Landing, I found a small force of Foster's men who were doing a sort of picket duty.

On explaining my mission and showing my pass to the officer in charge, he kindly loaned me a horse and took charge of my horse, which I had left on the opposite side of the river.

I arrived at Grahamville about two or three o'clock in the afternoon and found but three or four families in the town, the able-bodied men being absent in the Confederate Army. The town had been visited only by a small force of our army.

On inquiry I learned that the object of my visit lived at another town, four miles farther on, on the Savannah road. When nearing my destination, I discovered a violent thunderstorm approaching which threatened to drench me if I did not at once secure shelter. I first came to a church, then several negro houses, then to a neat residence lying about one hundred yards from the main road. Here I saw a gentleman sitting on the front porch, or as the people of the South call it, the gallery, and a beautiful walk leading up to the house.

A shed stood at the opposite side of the road under which to hitch horses, and as the storm was ready to break upon me, I hastily hitched my horse here, and walked toward the house to ask shelter during the storm, and to make further inquiries, when to my surprise I met a most beautiful young lady, who, however, was dressed decidedly "dishabille," she having on apparently but two garments, the names of which, I, being young and unmarried and having no large sisters at home, was unable to state. This young lady, having her head down to protect her face from the already falling rain, did not see me, and in my bashfulness, I could not think of a way to avoid her. She had in her hand a long stick on which was a large snake which was still wriggling. On seeing me she dropped her burden and ran to the house and disappeared within. The rain was now falling in torrents and there was nothing for me to do but to continue on to the porch, where sat the old gentleman. He invited me in out of the rain and asked me to assist him to go in as he could not move without help.

On inquiring for the residence of Captain Stevenson, I was told that this was the place and he was the man. At once I surmised that the young lady with the snake was the Miss Mollie of Dr. Stokesberry's story.

I then presented my letter of introduction from the worthy doctor and was received as an old friend might be. As soon as the rain slacked somewhat, he sent a negro to care for my horse, they insisting on my remaining with them for the night.

Then ensued a long conversation concerning the war and Dr. Stokesberry and his misfortunes. Not until supper was announced did Miss Mollie make her appearance, and I thought she was as much embarrassed as I was. The captain explained that while she was in her room dressing, a large snake had crawled out from under the house, a way snakes have in the South of moving about just before a storm, and then, as no negro was about, and he was unable to do himself, he had called her to kill it. I afterward measured it and found it to be five feet, eight inches long. It was of the species called in the South, house or chicken snakes, and not poisonous or dangerous to people. However, it was repulsive and horrible enough to scare most people.

I learned from the captain that he and all the remaining families were about at their last resources for supplies. He stated that notwithstanding his twenty years residence in the South, he had never become accustomed to the use of corn-bread. He said he had so far been able to keep on hand some wheat flour and occasionally (thanks to the blockade runners) a little coffee, but that now their supply was nearly exhausted, and although he had a few greenbacks saved up, all communications being cut off, he did not know how he would be able to replenish his store room.

It so happened that at the time Wheeler's men had visited them, he happened to have in a back field a lot of sweet potatoes not harvested, also that his hogs running in the woods were so wild that the raiders did not find all of them. A little corn had also been concealed so that they were able to get along up to this time. If he had been able to go to Savannah or Hilton Head, he would have been able to get along as he was a man of the world and I think he would have been successful in providing for the family.

He was a much better informed man than most of the planters, thereby being better enabled to meet the inevitable when it came. He had been injured while rounding Cape Horn, twenty-three years previously, having both legs crushed and never entirely recovering from the accident. After the breaking out of the war, his old injury became worse, and although he was now sixty years of age, he would probably have been required to shoulder a musket as a home guard but for this injury.

Dr. Stokesberry had, ten years before, given Miss Mollie a negro girl as a waiting maid. This was the only black person they had ever owned, but always kept a hired negro man to do the drudgery. He had kept a store until the breaking out of the war prevented his restocking the store. Since the closing of the store, he had simply sat in his easy chair and discussed the war with his neighbors. I remained with these good people for two days and, after the shyness and novelty of our first introduction had worn off, had several friendly and pleasant conversations with Miss Mollie.

She had asked me if I thought I could take some of their money and purchase and send to them some flour, meat, coffee, and some dry goods. I told her I would try but that the worst trouble would be in getting the goods hauled to her place from Boyd's Landing. She replied that she knew of an old mule that could be got for the purpose and their old faithful negro man would bring them up.

This being arranged, I returned to Beaufort, where I laid the matter before General Howard, and at his suggestion, General Saxton gave me a permit to send out the required articles. Some of the headquarters officers joked me about the matter and suggested that I call on Colonel Conklin A.Q.M.[3] and get some sanitary luxuries, which hint I acted upon. Colonel Conklin kindly permitted me to carry off a good back load of dainties, on my statement that it was for the good of the cause.

Twenty years later I met Colonel Conklin in Nebraska and introduced to him, "the cause."

PART II

The Campaign of the Carolinas

24

First Day

With steeds ungoverned, from the course I swerve;
Thoughts past control are whirling me along.

ON FEBRUARY 1, 1865, the army was stripped for another great march—this was to be an entirely different march from that first made through the State of Georgia, from "Atlanta to the Sea." On that march the soldiers did not appear to have any particular ill feeling or spirit of vindictiveness against the citizens of that great state, further than as Georgia was a part of the Confederacy, which all believed must be crushed before a peace could be expected and they be permitted to return to their homes.[1]

The entire army, and in fact the whole North, charged South Carolina with being responsible for the war and seemed to think that a severe punishment should be inflicted upon that state. It seemed to me that I could see a grim determination on their faces that indicated trouble was brewing. I may say also that in conversation with prisoners on the previous march, we often heard a wish expressed by them, that when we got into South Carolina, we would make the people of that state feel that, "He who will dance, must also pay the piper."

The luxuries that had been enjoyed by the army during the past forty days had to be given up, wagons were packed only with necessities. Knapsacks were again lightened, tents left behind, the sick and wounded left in hospitals and all, individually and collectively, felt that this was to be the grand closing march of the war. Having been so successful in the past, they believed themselves invincible in the future.[2]

I verily believe that if this army had existed in 1861 with their present commanders and their past experience, the war would have been closed in sixty days.

But while they all felt thus, they did not overlook the fact that the enemy had also gained experience, and they, as well as the enemy, now knew that they had "foes worthy of their steel."

I had at this time a bad felon [a painful abscess or infection at the end of a finger] on the middle finger of the right hand, which prevented me from using that hand if I should have occasion to use my revolver.

The 15th and 17th Corps each took separate roads, and I was ordered by General Howard to take with me one of the scouts and accompany the 15th, now commanded by General Logan, through the day and at night to cross over to the Column of the 17th Corps, where General Howard's headquarters would be, with such dispatches as General Logan, or General Sherman, might wish to send.[3]

I selected our new scout, Sergeant John A. White, partly for the reason that I wanted to initiate him, and partly because he and I had been mess mates and bunk mates in the earlier part of the war: had been taken prisoners together by General For[r]est, had escaped together, and when we were about to be recaptured by reason of my leg giving out, which took from me all hope of escape, he refused to abandon me, although he could have escaped by running and I strongly urged him to do so. I knew from experience the metal he was made of and I wanted to give him a little experience in scouting at this stage of the game.[4]

As we passed up, I noticed the 17th Wisconsin Infantry at the roadside, with their guns stacked, waiting to fall in line at their proper place. I was somewhat acquainted in that regiment and, seeing an Irish lieutenant of Company K, whom I knew, rode to him saying: "Well, Jim, we're off, and I want to say good-bye to you as we may not meet again." He stepped towards me and, taking me by the hand, said, "Good-bye, George, be a good boy and take care of yourself." I had forgotten my sore finger and did notice that he was somewhat intoxicated until he got hold of my hand and gave it a squeeze. I tried to release my hand, but the more I tried, the tighter he squeezed, saying all the time, "Be a good boy and take good care of yourself." The pain was so great that I fell from my horse and it was sometime before I could proceed. I can even now at times imagine that I feel his grip.

We soon overtook the head of the column and passed on to the advance, where we rode for a time, but this soon became monotonous, and we two started ahead. By riding fast we soon gained a couple of miles on them but saw no one until we came to McPhersonville, where we saw a mounted Rebel cross the road. There was not an inhabitant left in the town. There were several towns in South Carolina just back of tidewater that resembled this one. The houses would be built along the side of the road, ten to twenty rods apart. Thus a town of forty or fifty families would be strung along for nearly a mile. There would be but one store, which would also be a post office, a grocery, and perhaps a bakery, combined. The natural growth of trees would not be cut down, so it was really a town in the woods. These houses were as a rule owned and occupied by planters whose plantations were but a few miles distant or were down in the malarial districts of the sea islands and were used solely as a summer resort. They were often quite attractive and comfortable. There would generally be a church and sometimes a select school or small academy nearby.

The soldier we had seen acted as though he was trying to lead us in a trap. We took some chances in rushing him but he proved to be a straggler or a deserter, or possibly he may have been a solitary scout sent out to watch the movements of our army. At any rate we lost him in the woods and passed on. In cases like this we could always feel confident that if we got into a scrap, the advance guard would soon come to our assistance. The roads in this part of the state were on ground nearly dead level, the trees being cut out and removed to the width of sixty-six feet, and we were enabled to see long distances, and although the rainy season had commenced and considerable water was on the ground as there had been little or no travel over the roads for a year or two, they were not cut up and the traveling was good. However, after a heavy wagon train or a battery of artillery had passed over them, they would become almost impassable for teams and in many cases had to be corduroyed by the Pioneer Corps.[5] The infantry, however, had no trouble as they could easily go to the right or left of the road and find good footing in the woods. The land was quite poor and we found very few plantations, and only those of the poorer classes, until we got two or three days march up the country, where it grew better and the planters appeared to be more wealthy.

After leaving McPhersonville, we rode on for about a mile when we saw in the distance a group of perhaps a dozen people, who, all but one, dodged into the woods. The one stood in line and near to a big tree. I said to White, "Let me show you how near I can shoot to that man." I elevated my revolver with my left hand and fired. The man then made signs of peace and we rode forward to them and found that they were refugee negroes with their luggage on their heads. The one whom I fired at showed me where my bullet had struck, which was about eight feet above his head. The distance we estimated was about one-fourth of a mile. I mention this incident simply to show the power of those "Colt Navys."

We ran into the enemy's pickets near Hickory Hill Post Office, about fifteen miles from Pocat[a]ligo. This was a point where the column was to camp for the night and we awaited the arrival of General Howard's headquarters a distance of perhaps six or seven miles.

25

Crossing the Creek

In heaps the unhappy dead lie on the strand
of Salamis, and all the neighboring shores.

THE NEXT DAY, which was Candlemas Day (February 2nd), the scouts rode at the advance of the 17th Corps. There was a small squadron of cavalry, closely followed by the advance guard of the infantry, then the main column. We joined the cavalry and soon ran into the rear guard of the enemy, who, not being strong enough to give us a fight, tried to delay us by laying ambuscades and in other ways obstructing our progress. We had to flank them out of their position repeatedly, which somewhat delayed the main column, which repeatedly ran into our heels. General Howard became impatient at these delays and several times sent an aide to the front with orders to "Not stop to fight them, but run over them, kick them out of the way," etc., etc. This was all very well, theoretically, but as the enemy outnumbered our mounted advance, we were frequently compelled to maneuver and wait the arrival of the infantry advance.

About 11 o'clock A.M. we came to a small creek heavily lined with bushes beyond which the Confederates made a stand. We asked the infantry to simply hold them there, while the cavalry started to flank them on our left, and the scouts on the right. We found a ford a quarter of a mile to our right where we crossed and aimed to drop into the enemy's rear, when we were to commence firing and the infantry were to push forward, and together we would bag the entire lot. We got somewhat separated in the undergrowth and I hurried forward to join my friends, whom I thought I could see, but they proved to be the Rebel rear guard in retreat. I got within four rods of them before I discovered my mistake. They were also probably deceived by my grey coat. An officer called to me to come up, or come on, but I pretended not to be able to hear him distinctly and gradually worked my way to the cover of a large tree. The scouts and cavalry soon arrived and relieved me from my predicament. This was a case where my Rebel uniform saved my "bacon"—but for it, I may have got a dozen bullets at short range.

After getting up on the level open timberland again, we could see the Rebel rear guard a quarter of a mile away, retreating only as fast as we advanced. When we would stop, they would do the same; when we advanced, they would retreat. We could see away in the distance an angle in the road that the larger body of the enemy had disappeared behind, leaving one man who was several rods in their rear, when a courier came up from our rear with the order to "stop one hour for dinner." We halted and the Rebs halted. Our men withdrew to one side of the road in the shelter of the trees to feed the horses from their nose bags and eat a lunch themselves. One of the boys had taken my horse aside to feed him while I remained in the road to watch the enemy. I stood there some time gnawing a cracker, when one of the boys asked what the "John" was doing. I answered, "Simply standing there, watching us." Then someone said, "Give him a shot." Then it was, I did one of the many foolish things of my life. I elevated my gun and fired, and the Rebel pointed with his hand, evidently showing me where my bullet went. I explained this to the boys, and while doing so, the John fired at me, the bullet going about twenty feet to my left and above. Our boys then said, "It is but fair for you to show him where his bullet went." I did so, then the boys urged me to try again, which I did, he showing me as before the course of my bullet, on the other side of him. He then returned my second shot getting a little closer to me. This was repeated till all my shots (ten) were exhausted. Our boys came as near me as was safe, encouraging and tantalizing me. Along toward the last I became convinced that "Mr. John" was misrepresenting to me the course of my bullets, and I commenced using my own judgment instead of his signals. Our boys stood so close to me that I could not deceive him in like manner, even if I had been so inclined, without their knowing it, which they no doubt would have characterized as unfair and dishonorable. In the meantime my adversary's bullets were coming uncomfortably close to me, and I would have willingly "swapped" places with the meanest "bummer" in the army. Then I discovered that I had but one more load in my gun and said, "I will give him this last one and give him a chance to return it, then while I retire to reload, if there are any of you want some of this, you can have it in my place." I then took very careful aim and fired and thought I could see him waver, but he did not fall from his horse. He did not return this last shot but rode around the angle of the road and disappeared.

In South Carolina in 1866,[1] I met some of these same Confederates, from whom I learned that I had hit him with my last shot in his left side just below the shoulder, but that it was not a serious wound. In those days we called such escapades "glory," but I now look upon it as "damphoolishness."

On February 3rd, the scouts had some business to the left oblique, after which we rode toward the main column, where we heard a severe engagement in progress. We found a brigade here seriously engaged in trying to force a crossing over the Salkahatchie River at River's Bridge.[2] At this point the banks and river bottom were overflowed with rapidly running water from ankle to waist deep. The bridge had been burned and at the river proper was over against the opposite bank of dry ground. The enemy had thrown up breastworks and were making it mighty hot for our men. The brigade had stripped themselves of all surplus trappings and started in to wade. As the fire from the enemy grew warmer, they commenced taking shelter behind trees and would by rapid firing keep the enemy's heads down behind their works, while our men would gain a more advanced position where they in turn would hold the fort till the others came up and gained still further in advance. This continued until only the river and breastworks separated them from the enemy. Then all forced the Rebs to keep down, while a few men with axes stepped out and cut down trees, falling them so as to form foot bridges across the river, which was here but thirty or forty feet wide. When these bridges were ready, a few crossed and the enemy "skedaddled."

The brigade had thus been standing in the water for over six hours. On arriving at the post office, "River's Bridge," a good plantation house from which we could overlook the scene of battle, I saw some wounded being brought in, among whom I recognized some of my old regiment, who informed me that the brunt of the battle had fallen upon our old brigade, the 32nd Wisconsin and the 25th Indiana, under General Mower. They told me our loss was exceedingly heavy, many of the wounded by reason of being unable to gain shelter, drowned after being hurt. I asked permission of General Howard to remain that afternoon and assist in taking care of the wounded, to which he cheerfully consented. I here learned that our regiment lost more men killed and wounded in this insignificant battle than at all the other battles they were engaged in, combined, being about eighty-four killed and two hundred wounded.[3]

26

Mr. New

Was wont with her chaste voice to supplicate
For her dear father an auspicious fate

THE NEXT DAY General Howard sent back eighty wagons loaded with wounded to Pocateligo [Pocotaligo] and called for a scout to pilot them. I asked him as a favor that I be permitted to go, on account of being acquainted with so many of the sufferers, which request was readily granted.

It was very painful trip, for both the wounded and myself. From time to time during the two days of the trip, I would look into the different wagons trying to say something cheerful, or to give them water, till it made my heart sick. Many of these men died later in hospital at Hilton Head, among whom was my very good friend Sergeant Ben Sheldon.[1]

General Swayne, who lost a leg at this engagement, was of this party, but I do not remember having seen him there.[2]

We took a different and shorter road than the one used by either of the corps, because of the fact that those roads were badly cut up by heavy trains.

After bidding the boys good-bye at Pocotaligo, many of them for the last time, I returned to the army by still another road, farther south, and got into a section traveled over by a portion of Kilpatrick's cavalry, where I found destitution which made me wish I had never heard of war. I had provided for myself at Pocataligo, my saddlebags full of rations and a couple of feeds of oats for my horse. I left about noon and made about thirty miles that evening, and stayed that night with an old couple who had not been entirely stripped of their provisions. The next morning at daybreak I started a little after sunrise and called at a home to inquire about the road, but found no one there, although the door was open. Looking across the road in an old slashing where some cavalry had camped two or three nights before, I saw near a fire a woman and two small children. I rode over to them to make my inquiries, where I found them gathering up the cobs from which the horses had gnawed the corn, leaving a few grains at either end. She informed me that this was all she had to keep her children from starving. I think I need not add that my horse and I went without dinner that day. I could not have eaten a mouthful for thinking of those poor hungry children.[3] I came to the conclusion, as did General Sherman, that "War is Hell."

I arrived at headquarters on the evening of the 6th. The next morning the scouts were separated into two or three parties and sent in different directions on separate errands. One of the new scouts was sent with me ahead of the army in a right oblique direction along the line of railroad leading from Charleston to Augusta to see if we could learn of the presence of the enemy in force. About ten o'clock we came to a fine plantation owned by a gentleman by the name of G. W. New. He was at home. He was about seventy-two or seventy-five years of age, about six feet two inches in height, and was as fine a specimen of a Southern gentleman as I ever met. I told him who we were and he answered our questions frankly.

This new scout then rudely demanded of him if he had any firearms and was answered, "No." I made the scout shut up in short order as this was not our policy or purpose. This was one of the new scouts who had recently been assigned to our corps. He had early proved to be more of a forager than a scout and a very impudent and cruel forager at that. I reported this to General Howard and he was at once sent back to his command. Our corps of scouts did not approve of this method of serving our country. It was not policy, it was not gentlemanly, and it was not the proper course to pursue to obtain the object for which we were sent.[4]

There were about twenty-five negroes in the yard, which the old gentleman informed me, were born and reared on the plantation. He was aware they would be set free and seemed very much pained to reflect what would now become of them, as he did not seem to think they would be competent to care for themselves.[5]

I asked him how he was provided for meat and he took me to the smokehouse and showed me perhaps two tons of smoked meat. I told him that the army would arrive in an hour or two and would take all his meat and corn (of which he had three or four thousand bushels in the cribs nearby), and that he had better send his negroes to hide some of his meat in a swamp for his own use when the army had passed. He replied that he could not do it because if he was asked if this was all he had, he would be compelled to answer that he had a little concealed for his own use. My heart went out to him and I thought of a plan, whereby I could save for him something and still preserve his truthfulness. I then went into the yard and ordered the negroes to bring me from the smokehouse twelve or fifteen good hams. I then caused them to be thrown into a corner of the parlor and had the carpet ripped up and thrown over them in a manner that looked as if the house had already been ransacked, and all the negroes being present, I said to him, "These hams are mine. Do not touch them nor tell the army where they are." I then turned to the negroes, telling them that I should return in the evening, and if I did not find the hams, I would hold them personally responsible for them and would take that much out of their hides. After dismissing the servants, the old gentleman told me that his eyesight was very poor and that he had some time previously secured a pair of very valuable gold bowed spectacles, but fearing that some of the "bummers" would take them, he had his wife hide them in her bosom. He asked me if I thought it was safe for him to put them on while the army was passing. After stating that we wanted to see them and reflecting a moment, I told him he had better let them remain where they were.

He told me that there was another matter troubling him. That he had told my comrade that he had no firearms, when as a matter of fact he did have a small silver mounted Smith & Wesson, Caliber 22, revolver that had been a present to him, that was now concealed down in the swamp, that he wished to get and give to me. I told him that it could be of no use to me or harm to the army to let it remain where it was. He said no, that it might get him into trouble—that others might make the same demand on him—that he had lived thus far as a truthful man and wished to die as such. He then got it and presented it to me, and I accepted it with the understanding that if he was alive at the close of the war, he should receive it back again.

I will here add, *en passant*, that in August 1865 I had his name engraved on the revolver and returned it to him by the hands of my scout comrade, Joe Bedoll, who in the meantime had been promoted and assigned to duty in that vicinity.

While here, I heard of seventeen fine horses that were concealed several miles from there. (Of course this news came from negroes.) We succeeded in finding them and appropriated six of the best ones. In the evening we returned to the plantation of Mr. New and found that the foragers had been there and taken all of his corn except some scattering ears, all of his meat from the smokehouse, and had ransacked the house but, fortunately, did not find my hams. The old gentleman and his wife were there; he was wearing his spectacles. I stripped off the carpet and told him that in "token of the fact that I had found an honest man, I wished to present him with fifteen fine hams." Tears ran down their aged cheeks and I had to turn away to hide my emotion. He insisted on our remaining with him that night, but I could not think of staying there and assisting them to eat up their scanty provisions.

Mr. New dwelt at some length on his family affairs. He said he had but two children, boys, one of whom was a surgeon in the Confederate Army. The other one had just graduated from a law school in 1860 and at the Secession Convention at Charleston had made his maiden speech, which was pronounced by those competent to judge, to be equal to any effort ever made by John C. Calhoun. Then he added with a sigh, "Poor boy, he is now a hopeless maniac in the Hospital for the Insane at Columbia. I shall never see him again."

I mention this and like events that the reader may know that the scouts had a better opportunity to learn and understand the people of the South than the average soldier.

27

Miss Virginia

Two women stood before my eyes
. . . .
With more than mortal majesty they moved,
Of peerless beauty: sisters too, they seemed.

FOR A COUPLE OF DAYS, the scouts were kept on the extreme right of the army, near the South Edisto River, watching to see if the enemy should attempt to throw a force across to harass our rear. Nothing of the kind occurred, however. On the 10th, we moved up to the South Edisto at a point nearly due north of Midway, where we arrived in advance of the army, with the exception of one solitary Indian, of the Menomonee tribe in Wisconsin. His name was John Law (his Indian name was "Meeses," probably a corruption of Moses), and he was a member of Company K, 17th Wisconsin Infantry. I had known him in my boyhood days and had often played with him at shooting arrows, throwing tomahawks, swimming, and canoe racing. He was then a very pleasant and agreeable companion, but since he had grown up, he had become morose, unsociable, and misanthropical. The captain of his company, had, sometime since, turned him adrift to shift for himself. Law had somehow secured possession of an old-time Kentucky rifle, with which he made every effort to kill Rebels. He seemed to kill for the sake of killing, not because he knew or cared a fig about the cause.

This Indian had arrived before us by a few minutes, and as the rear guard of the enemy retreated down the grade towards the bridge, he fired, killing one of them. The man lay in plain sight of us and I asked Law how he had been killed. He answered, "Me kill 'em." I then remembered hearing of his murderous inclinations and asked him how many he had killed. He showed me his gun stock with a fresh notch cut in it, and I counted sixteen notches. I asked him if he had killed that many, but instead of answering, he turned away and did not reply. A few days later, I inquired of his company officers if they thought he had killed that number and they replied that they had no doubt of it.

The army now arrived and commenced operations to effect a crossing, but did not succeed until the next day. Headquarters camp was made near here, and towards night, Amick came in and reported to us that late that afternoon he had passed through "Graham's Turnout," a station four miles to our rear on the Augusta Railroad, when the rear of the 15th Corps was passing. That he had met two or three young ladies who had expressed fear that some stragglers might return and destroy the town or do like damage, and had invited him to return at night with a few agreeable friends and they would get up a small party and entertain them to the extent of their ability. They candidly admitted that their object was to secure protection against stragglers and negroes.

I was the only one who would accompany him, the rest fearing a trap or trick of some kind.

We arrived at the village about 8 o'clock P.M., and found things in a bad mess. The house of the ladies in question, who were daughters of a Mr. McMillen, who was said to be the superintendent of the Charleston & Augusta R.R., had been burned and a portion of their household goods was scattered around the yard. They reported to us that a man claiming to be a major of a regiment in the 15th Corps in command of a small squad of men had arrived about dark and claimed to have written orders from General Logan to burn this particular house and none other. He had given them twenty minutes to remove their belongings, but would not allow them to remove the piano. Negroes assisted them in hastily removing their effects, when he set fire to the building and left the town. The house had stood in the center of a fine large lawn and must have been a fine one. The furniture and household goods as they lay scattered about indicated that they belonged to the aristocracy of the country. About half a dozen young ladies were congregated around the fire, together with a host of negroes in the background. One of the ladies, a daughter of the proprietor, was carrying on at a terrible rate, abusing and denouncing the Yankees as none but an educated Southern woman could do. The others were trying to quiet her but without success.[1]

We did not stop to inquire into the cause of all this destruction, but gathered up a crowd of negroes and had all the effects removed to a vacant building nearby, where I placed an old negro over them as a watchman. One of the young ladies, whose name I have forgotten, but whose name should be preserved in history because of her good sense and presence of mind, invited all ladies and Yankees to repair to her house, where, "Although, she could not entertain us as well as she wished, she would at least make us welcome." About this time the emotional young lady, whose name we learned was Virginia McMillen, having exhausted her vituperation, went off into hysterics and a partial fainting spell. We carried her to the home of the sensible young lady, who for want of her true name, I will call Miss Fanny. There she was placed on the lounge in the back parlor, where she for hours kept up her denunciations of the Yankees.

We were here informed of the cause of their trouble. The major had stated to the ladies that he had, some months previous, been a prisoner and that while being removed with a train load of others, to another prison, the train had stopped opposite the house in question. The prisoners had asked permission of the Confederate officer in charge to go to the well in the yard for water. After several prisoners had obtained a drink and he was in the act of drinking, this identical Miss Virginia had come out and snatched the gourd from him and said that "No Yankee should drink, and thus pollute her well." Miss Virginia denied this to us but Miss Fanny told us confidentially that there might possibly be some truth in the allegation. Miss Virginia's sister, Miss Lillian, I think her name was, was present and was strong in her disapproval of the conduct of her sister.

This denunciation at last became unbearable to me, and as Amick was enjoying himself with three or four ladies, I did not wish to disturb him, so I quietly went out and was bridling my horse to return to camp when Miss Fanny detected my movements and came out and urged me to remain. She was soon joined by Amick and all the ladies, who also insisted. I told them I could not remain and listen to such language. Miss Fanny said, "If you will remain, we will make her stop if we have to stuff a pillow in her mouth."

Amick has since often told me that I should go back and marry Miss Virginia and subdue some of her rebellious spirit, but I thought it best to leave that job to someone of a thicker skin than mine.[2]

28

Mascots

He lacks not much who lacks a grave.

WE ARRIVED AT camp early next morning and found General Howard had issued an order for the scouts to be ready to march up the river to the left to see if we could find a private bridge or ferry where troops could be put across to surprise and capture the Confederates who were concentrated at the principal bridges.

After going a few miles, we found a road, not much traveled, leading toward the river and found, on arriving there, a private bridge and causeway without any of the enemy in sight to prevent our passage.

One man was sent back to the nearest troops to notify them of this discovery. The balance of us crossed over to reconnoiter. We soon came to the forks of the road, the main one leading straight north, the other following down the stream. Dawson and I were sent down this latter road to picket it, while the others were to go out on the northern one to see the situation. They were to signal us by a shot when they returned. Dawson and I rode out nearly half a mile and dismounted to listen for sounds and our friends' signal.

Dawson and I had had for some time a little difference between us that left a "coldness," and this being a good opportunity, we entered into explanations that so occupied our minds that we almost forgot our duty. We had sat there perhaps an hour, holding our bridle reins, when suddenly we heard the tramp of horses' feet, from towards the enemy. Instantly I sprang into the saddle and, looking through the bushes, across a sharp bend of the road about four rods away, saw a group of Rebel cavalry, or more probably a general officer with his staff and body guard, as they were well dressed in clean uniforms. They, on seeing me, came to a halt, and I drew a gun to fire at them, more to give the alarm to Amick's party than from a desire to kill. Dawson's horse was a very nervous one and our springing up so quickly made him so restless that Dawson had a very difficult time mounting. I waited till he had regained his saddle and then fired directly into the mass of cavalry, and then we lit out for the forks of the road, expecting to be followed by them. I never learned the effects of my shot, but this I know, that the party immediately returned from whence they came. This was another time that my Confederate uniform saved me, because we were in plain sight of them and no doubt they would have charged before we were ready if I had worn blue clothing.

I have always thought that they returned to the force in front of General Howard and reported that the Yankees had effected a crossing above them, as they soon after left his front, enabling him to cross without a loss like that of Salkiehatchie.

Probably there never was an army on a long march that was as cheerful and self-confident as the one which marched from Atlanta to Goldsboro.[1] The ranks were reasonably well closed up but no rigid rules of discipline were enforced to compel the men to march elbow to elbow. On the contrary, the men were allowed to deploy to the right or left of the road to suit their convenience and take advantage of the best ground. Their distance was always well preserved so that in the event of a surprise, they could instantly spring to their places and be ready for anything. On the march there was a constant chatter of conversation going on along the entire line. One group would discuss, wisely or otherwise, as to the destination and success of the campaign. Another perhaps, as to the probabilities of the foragers returning laden with hams and poultry, while still another, and perhaps the larger number, would be cracking jokes at some unfortunate who had fallen in the mud, lost his chicken, or some other mishap.

Throughout the army, "sells" were always in order. In camp, on the march, or in battle, woe be to the man who asked a question. One had only to ask a question, no matter how innocent, harmless, or necessary it might be, and he would get an answer that would shave his whiskers.

In imitation of the 8th Wisconsin, which had a live eagle as a mascot, nearly every company and battery in this army had a mascot of some kind. It might be a goat, a pig, a dog, a cat, a monkey, a parrot, a rooster, or even the smallest donkey to be found, and these mascots were kept with the company wherever they went. Roosters were the most plentiful, by reason of the fact that they were the most easily obtained. They soon became so tame that they considered themselves at home wherever the company halted, if only for a few minutes. Cock fighting soon became the leading amusement of the army and many a dollar was lost and won by these pets.

Dogs were the next most plentiful of these animals. Companies and regiments soon became known by the peculiarity of their dogs. Perhaps the greatest variety of dogs ever collected was by the Army of the Carolinas.

During an effort to secure a crossing of the South Edisto by one of these corps fronts, the road approaching the bridge had been filled with fallen trees, with the enemy behind breastworks. Our skirmishers were working their way through obstructions when a shot from the enemy hit one of these dogs, which raised a howl that could be heard for a mile. Immediately five thousand voices, Reb and Yank, were raised in a yell that caused everyone to laugh heartily. Such events tended to enliven the soldiers and make these campaigns a pleasure instead of a hardship.

29

Rain

THE NEXT DAY after the army crossed the South Edisto, the scouts were separated again. Dawson and I went together in a left oblique direction. On the Carolina March, the scouts and foragers did not, and could not, go as far from the columns as they could, and did, in Georgia because there was a much stronger force of the enemy in our front.

We found nothing of note until about 2 o'clock P.M., when we were passing through an old field grown up to bushes, we saw two Confederate infantrymen coming towards us who did not see us. We waited till they got to the proper distance and halted them and demanded their surrender. They threw down their arms at our demand and came towards us, and we started to secure the weapons, but six men under charge of a sergeant of one of our cavalry regiments, who had been watching us, went forward and picked up the arms. Among them was a fine silver mounted six-inch navy revolver, which I demanded of him on the ground that we were the captors. He refused to give it up and his men seconded him in his claims, on the ground that he was entitled to it by right of might. I had to submit to this injustice but a few days later I met him with his regiment and renewed my demand in the presence of his officers. I had thought of this act of tyranny and injustice and had become very angry. Boy-like, I had more temper than sense in those days, and I then challenged him to show his courage with his choice of weapons. His captain placed me in arrest and it might have gone hard with me had not Colonel Conklin, A.Q.M. of General Howard's staff, happened to pass just then and released me. I never met this cowardly sergeant again, but had decided in my own mind that if ever I did see him away from his command, I would have that revolver if I had to use my gun, and I was angry and young and foolish enough to have done it.

As I have before stated, it was an unwritten law in the army, that "To the victor (or captor) belongs the spoils," and none but a coward disputed it.

On the 12th of February, the 17th Corps swung more to the right aiming for Orangeburg on the north, or main branch of the Edisto River, where we expected some more serious opposition. However, a crossing was effected without much of a fight.

Even at this time the rank and file of the army thought our destination was to be Charleston, but on the next morning when the heads of columns were again pointing north, we all felt that it was to be Columbia.[1]

The afternoon and evening of the 13th were very rainy and we all got very wet, and for some reason our wagon did not arrive that night, so we did not get a chance to dry ourselves and our weapons. The next morning the scouts were routed out early and started before daylight. We passed our advance pickets at first light of day, and had gone but about two hundred yards when we suddenly ran into the Confederates' pickets. They had been stationed at the end of a long lane. They fired a few shots and retreated down the lane. When they had gone about a hundred yards, they apparently discovered that we were few in number and concluded to give us a scrap. All except their commanding officer fired and retreated pell-mell. Our boys had scattered to the right and left for shelter, but when I saw this officer standing there bidding us defiance, I thought I would like to exchange a shot with him, and so I took a position in the middle of the lane to do so. I aimed and snapped every one of my shots and not one would explode. He did the same with the same result, so it proved a bloodless battle. When he had tried his last shot and failed, he gave me a fine military salute, which I returned, and then retreated. I would like to meet him again and sample some "moonshine." Amick said I was a fool for taking such chances and I suppose I was.

This lane was nearly a mile long and cleared on both sides. The road declined gradually for about half the distance, then gradually ascended to the woods beyond. We halted here till the infantry came up when we were sent to the left to see about roads, etc. When we returned two hours later, we found a division of men deployed and advancing about two-thirds of the way to the woods, where the enemy was discovered in some force. Preparations were being made for a battle if the Johns would stand.

We found General Howard at the entrance of the lane, and he sent us to the right front to deliver a dispatch to General Wood. The whole of our route was in open land, but a strong skirmish line was in our front and heavy columns close to our rear. After leaving our horses in a depression for safety, we started for a fence that was in good view of what we expected would be the charge. This fence was parallel to our line of march and at right angles to the line of Confederate works. When we got near it, we saw one or more of our stragglers in nearly every fence corner. Suddenly the enemy turned loose an eight- or twelve-pound solid shot at this fence, which caught a few of the top rails, then on a ricochet took a few more rails farther along, then again still farther down the line. I never heard if anyone was hurt but it was amusing to see the men "skedaddle" from that fence. I can see those rails flying yet.

The Rebels soon retreated without a battle and our column pursued its course and arrived at the Little Congaree River that night.

30

Pontoon Bridge on Congaree River

ON THE MORNING of the 16th, we rode from the 17th Corps to a point opposite Columbia, where we found General Sherman, Slocum, and Logan on the front porch of a house looking through their glasses at the city.[1] The 15th Corps was passing and Captain De Gress (Old Leather Breeches) was throwing an occasional shot from these twenty-pound popguns into the city.[2] We could see without a glass negroes and white men, probably citizens, with mules, horses, carts, and carriages moving about in great confusion. It looked to us like every sort of vehicle was being used to haul away cotton. When the first shell exploded over this part of the city, everyone cut loose his horse or mule and skedaddled, leaving the carts and cotton standing in the street.

During this time when the attention of the officers was drawn towards the city, there were dozens of stragglers from Logan's columns in the backyard helping themselves to the hams and chickens, and the lady of the house having discovered the depredations, came rushing towards the group of officers to enter a complaint. An aide de camp met her and she poured forth her lament in bitter tones and asked him to stop it. He listened calmly till she got through, then said, "Madam, you know *too well* where we are." Amick and I and probably other scouts saw and heard this distinctly. The lady accepted the situation and made no further complaint.

The bridge across the Congaree River had been burned and the stone piers still stood in the river. The river here was too wide to be spanned by the pontoon bridges, so the 15th Corps had hurried forward to the Saluda River, a tributary three miles above, to try to save a bridge, but it had been burned also.

Up the Saluda a quarter of a mile was a woolen mill still running, making goods for the Confederate Army. This factory was burned after permitting the operators to take away as much of the products as they could carry. Some historians in speaking of this event say that these operatives (women) were a forlorn and unintelligent lot of "crackers," but I noticed a lot of intelligent and bright-looking faces among the number. I think one's sympathies have much to do with the lens of one's spectacles.[3]

Across the river was an open field, perhaps forty rods wide, then woods. A road ran across the peninsula from the destroyed bridge, a half mile to another bridge across Broad River. The reader will understand that these two rivers form the Congaree River.

By the time we arrived at the Saluda, the pontoon train had arrived and the pontooneers soon had a few boats launched. While a regiment of troops kept the enemy concealed in the woods beyond, the pontoons soon landed a force of skirmishers across the river, who acted as sharp shooters to protect the pontooneers while they were building the bridge. They soon had a rope stretched across and the bridge commenced. I stood by and saw the whole work and never saw one built faster, before or since. It seemed to me that it was completed as fast as one would travel at a very slow walk. In the meantime, General Logan, who was superintending the work, had ordered his body guard and our scouts to be ready, and when the last plank was laid, to make a rush for the other bridge and save it if possible. He said we would be followed on double quick by the Infantry. As we were crossing, the skirmishers already across, charged the Rebels in the woods, but we soon passed them and flew to the bridge, intending to take every chance to save it.

The road leading to this bridge was cut down through a bank to the level of the bridge. When we arrived at the entrance, the retreating enemy were two thirds across it, with the bridge burning behind them. Large quantities of cotton and resin had been scattered along the bridge and the flames ran like a prairie fire. Inside of sixty seconds the entire bridge was ablaze.

In order to get a better view, we got to the riverbank above the bridge, with the hill behind us as a background. The distance from the river to the hill was but two or three rods, and some scattering trees were growing there. We could see the enemy on the opposite bank but the distance was too great for our weapons. Suddenly they turned loose on us two or three pieces of artillery. The shots passed through our group and went into the bank near us. This was such a surprise that I want to confess I never was more frightened in my life. We could not get out of the scrape and had to stand and take it for a few minutes, which seemed to me several hours, till "Leather Breeches" arrived with his battery, who soon put the enemy to flight. Fortunately they were all solid shots, at least none of them exploded and none of us were hurt.

The scouts then spent the balance of the day in reconnoitering the country up this peninsula.

There not being enough pontoons to span to both rivers at once, the entire right wing, the 15th and 17th Corps, had to cross the Saluda to this peninsula so as to use all of the pontoons of both Corps to span the Broad. This was accomplished by 12 o'clock next day and the scouts were among the first who crossed. While riding across, I counted and found there were seventy-eight pontoons and two improvised flat boats used in its construction. I do not remember the distance these pontoons were apart, but think they could not be less than twelve feet from center to center. This would make nine hundred seventy-two feet for the whole river.

31

Fire in Columbia

Though it is honest, it is never good
to bring bad news.

WHEN WE ARRIVED in the city, we found that it was full of cotton. Every
warehouse and cotton shed was full, and cotton was piled up in backyards;
many bales were in the streets and on the abandoned carts.

We found a beautiful city, the residence streets being lined with many
shade trees and ornamental fences.

In those days cotton was not baled with iron ties, as now, and during
the war jute bagging could not be obtained; consequently bales of cotton
were tied with wooden hoops or ropes. It seems that many negroes had,
after the departure of the Confederate forces from the city and before our
arrival, cut the hoops or ropes of many hundreds, perhaps thousands, of the
abandoned bales, in various parts of the city. When it was released from
these bonds, the cotton expanded to great dimensions and the extremely
high winds of that day and night carried it like so much drifting snow, till it
found lodgment in some tree or fence. When our army arrived in the city, it
looked like a heavy drifting snowstorm had fallen. Every conceivable object
that was capable of catching and holding a lock of cotton had done so.

I found quarters that night at the residence of an old gentleman, who had
invited me to remain as his guest. It seemed that many of the citizens preferred a Yankee as his guest as he was sort of protection against marauders.

There had been some fires during the day, but all in comparatively safe
places. General Howard had caused them to be extinguished as far as possible. About dark the city was as quiet as was Memphis at its most quiet time
during the war.

Sometime between nine and ten o'clock that night, I was aroused from a sound sleep by the cry of fire and had scarcely time to dress myself when the house I was in caught fire. On reaching the street, I saw that the city was doomed. The wind had increased to nearly fifty miles an hour. When the fire first started, I doubt if there was a hundred soldiers in the town, aside from those on guard, but within twenty minutes it was full of soldiers, who came from nearby camps, some from curiosity and others possibly for plunder.

At first, Generals Howard, Sherman, and Logan tried to stop the fire, but that being found impossible, they turned their attention to controlling the soldiers. The soldiers appeared to become frantic. It was known that large quantities of tobacco had been stored here for the Confederate government, and as tobacco had become a scarce luxury in our army, every effort was made by them to secure a supply. I, myself, saw Generals Sherman, Howard, Logan, and others try to turn this mass of soldiers back to their camp without success, until a regiment was brought in under arms who arrested all who did not escape.

I was told next morning that this regiment had twenty-two hundred soldiers under guard, all of whom were later released.

After the war there was several years of newspaper controversy over the question of who was responsible for the destruction of this fine city.[1] The Northern papers held that Hampton had set it on fire, and the Southern papers asserted that it was the Yankee Army. Two days after the fire I learned the origin of it, but for reasons known to all soldiers, refrained from reporting it. All of the scouts also learned it and for the same reason kept still.

I was at Charleston in 1866, at a time when this newspaper controversy was going on, and wrote a full account of it for publication in the Charleston *Courier*, but its manager refused to publish it. I then sent it to a prominent Northern paper and have never heard that it was published.

The facts were these, as told to us scouts by one of the parties concerned:

After dark on that night, one Joe McGath,[2] a private orderly of General _____, with a friend went to a house of ill fame and being admitted were soon driven out by a party of seven or eight cavalry soldiers, who claimed to belong to Kilpatrick's command. They in turn gathered a crowd of eighteen or twenty infantry soldiers and dispossessed the cavalry. These cavalrymen, not being able to regain possession, set fire to the building, and it being in the midst of the flying cotton, a few moments sufficed to place the fire beyond control.

On February 20th, the right wing left Columbia for Winnsboro. The army had had three days' rest and were in prime condition for marching, fighting, or whatever came their way.

Now an amusing thing occurred that all the Army of the Tennessee will remember.

At Columbia thousands of soldiers had each secured plug tobacco in lots of from ten to forty pounds. Each one had loaded up expecting to sell it to his less fortunate comrades, when away from the city. Soon after leaving their camps, these loads began to pull down on their knapsacks straps. If there is anything a soldier dislikes more than another, it is a heavy knapsack when on a march. Then began negotiations for barter or sale. The price started in at .50 per plug, then fell to .25 then to .10, with still no buyers. It was soon seen that the market was glutted. Overstocked, I think is the term used on the Board of Trade.

Then, as the straps pulled harder and the knapsacks grew heavier, each began to offer to others free tobacco. It was then discovered that all were in the same boat. All had tobacco to sell or give away; no one would accept it even as a gift. The idea of keeping this surplus until such time as the market improved was not to be thought of. Then began a lightening of their loads by throwing away all, but keeping just enough to supply each tobacco user till they would arrive at the next tobacco depot. Each began by simply throwing away a few plugs, but soon as the knapsacks were still too heavy, more was cast aside.

While the scouts, being in advance, did not see this extravagance and waste, I have heard many soldiers who were in the ranks say that one could have walked for ten miles, every step of which could have been made on a plug of tobacco. In modern parlance, there was tobacco to throw at the birds.

32

On to Camden

THE SCOUTS CROSSED the Catawba River on the 20th of February on a ferry boat before the pontoon bridge was ready for the army.

On either the 20th or 21st, we had been off to the right to see if any of the enemy were about. On returning to the territory ranged over by the foragers, we came to a fine mansion, the best we had seen in the South. On coming in sight, we saw a large number of foragers about the place, and on getting nearer, we saw smoke pouring out of the windows. We then learned that this was Wade Hampton's plantation.[1] I soon dismounted and made a rush for the house to secure something for a memento. As I reached the main entrance, a soldier came out of the blinding smoke with four ivory billiard balls. By this time the smoke was so dense in all parts of the mansion that one could not breathe in it. I asked the soldier to sell me one of those balls, but he would not part with one at any price. He told me I could rush in by holding my breath, turn to the right to a writing desk, and secure something, at least. After he described the situation inside, I took a full breath, went in, and felt along the wall till I came to a desk of some kind, and as my breath was now exhausted, my hand rested on some object which I grasped and brought out.

It proved to be a beautiful mahogany dust box, such as was used fifty years ago for the purpose that blotting paper is now used. I have that box on my desk now.

If General Wade Hampton had not proved himself such a brute, and later treated our Chief Duncan so shamefully, I should long ago have returned it to him with an explanation of how it came in my possession.

After crossing the Catawba, the 17th Corps took a due east course but soon ran into the Lynch Creeks. These creeks were at this point several in number, the land between the different branches being but little above ordinary high water mark. The rainy season had set in sometime before and the whole country was lob-lolly of mud. All bridges were carried away and the whole road had to be corduroyed or bridged for many miles. There was scarcely a dry spot on which men could lie down. This part of the army was seven days in moving as many miles.[2]

I remember seeing on the evening of the 21st, a temporary bridge that the men had built over one of these creek bottoms, thirty to forty rods long, on stilts, as the boys called them. The rapid running water under it was from two to three feet deep. A wagon train was on the bridge when the whole structure gave way and landed the train in the mud and water. How they were gotten out, I never learned.

On the morning of the 22nd, Washington's Birthday, one I shall always remember, the scouts were ordered to go south to Camden, General Francis Marion's old Revolutionary battleground, a distance of about twenty-four miles, and ascertain if Beauregard had left that place, and if not, to try to learn the number of his force there.

We left the army in the mud and water and soon found dryer ground. We had gone perhaps ten miles when I secured a fine cream-colored stallion, which I admired very much. The former owner did also, but I consoled him by leaving my horse in his stead, making an even "swap," as we called it. Perhaps he had another name for it.[3]

The horse was beautiful enough for a "Jigadier Brindle" to ride, and I speculated some as to which one of the generals I would present him to.

Not far beyond that, as Bob and I, who were riding in advance, came to a turn in the road which led up a lane, we saw a man in Confederate uniform, but without insignia of his rank, approaching us. It was our custom in like circumstances to show no alarm or concern, but to advance as though war was unknown. This, many times enabled us to secure information that could not otherwise be obtained.

The Confederate carried in his hand the most beautiful and valuable double-barreled shotgun I had ever seen, both barrels cocked. As we got near him, I saluted and bade him "Good morning." He returned the salute genteelly, but before he could commence asking us questions, I began to interrogate him, as to the roads, their condition, the whereabouts of the Yankees, etc., etc., and finally if General Beauregard still had his headquarters at Camden. He answered these questions readily and was just beginning to explain the movements of Beauregard when our main body of scouts under

Lieutenant McQueen made their appearance around the turn of the road. He took a good look at them and thought he recognized in McQueen an old acquaintance of his.

Without stopping to answer my question, he urged his horse forward saying, "I'll declare, there is my old friend Captain King." We permitted him to pass us but immediately followed, giving signals to the boys, who, of course, were facing us, to be cautious and pump him.

When he got nearly to the boys, he said, "How are you, Captain King, I did not expect to see you here." Then discovering his mistake, he said, "I beg your pardon, sir, I thought you were my old friend, Captain King." Now, if McQueen had had more experience as a scout, he would have entered into conversation with him and got all the information we wanted. Instead of that, he rode up to the Confederate and, grasping the shotgun, said, "Give me that gun." The man having the butt of the gun and McQueen the muzzle, both pulling, put his finger on the trigger and said, "Let loose of that gun, sir," and said it as though he meant it. I saw at once that he meant business, and that I must act immediately to save McQueen, so I moved up and, pushing a pistol within two inches of his face, ordered him to surrender. "Who to?" he asked. "To Uncle Sam," I replied. He then said, "All right, gentlemen, I would have done so sooner, but I thought you were some of Wheeler's thieves."

Had McQueen not made this bad break, we could have returned to headquarters at once and the government would have been saved several thousands of dollars which has been paid to me in small monthly stipends for what followed that day.[4]

One of the scouts returned to camp from this point with the prisoner, to take him to headquarters to pump as he bluntly refused to answer any more of our questions. We were then about ten miles from Camden. Some four miles further on, we met a negro who had just come from that town, who reported to us that Beauregard had left the place, going east. That there was about one hundred "hoss sojers" in town and that there were thirty homeguards stationed about one mile this side of Camden, but that three of them had gone to town, leaving but twenty-seven at the place as a picket guard. We could then have returned, as this evidence seemed reliable, but some inquisitive Yankee asked the darky, what those one hundred men were doing in town. He said they were waiting for a blacksmith to repair a wagon which they were guarding. He was then asked what was in the wagon, and replied that he did not know, but that it was "Mighty heabby, sah." We then speculated as to what it could be.

Here I must recall some camp rumors that we had been hearing for some days. First, that the Confederate government had been keeping their hoarded gold to the amount of several millions of dollars at Columbia. Second, that on the approach of Sherman's army, they had run it off, "in wagons."

This story with all its variations had been repeated so often that many had come to believe it. Some of our party suggested that this broken-down wagon might be one of those containing Confederate gold. This theory went like wildfire, and everyone was ready to try to secure it at any cost.

33

Wounded

The Assyrians came down like the wolf on the fold.

IT WAS PROPOSED that we approach the Rebel picket as near as possible, without being seen, then deploy to, say, ten-rod intervals, then charge. Each giving orders as though each was in command of a regiment. Then after stampeding the pickets to rush for the town, shooting and yelling the whole way and try to stampede the "gold guards," and run off the booty. No sooner was it moved than it was seconded and carried unanimously.

We compelled the negro, much against his will, to accompany us to show us exactly where the pickets were located. We soon arrived at the foot of a rise of ground where the darky showed us the pickets. They were stationed among the trees in the open pine woods, at the top of a hill, and were about one hundred fifty yards distant.

Our six scouts here deployed, as proposed, and were advancing when we came upon two ladies who were crossing the main road by a path, or were stationed there as videttes. At any rate, when they saw our revolvers ready for action, they began to scream. I, being nearest them, rode to and told them they need not be alarmed, to pass along and they would be safe, etc., but they would not stop screaming, which apparently caused some commotion on the hill.

The boys, seeing we were discovered, raised the yell and charged, I among the rest. The pickets were so panic stricken, that they left their post, leaving the most of their guns. I was to the left of their camp, where I saw a small fenced field not far distant, and an old man climbing over the fence. I rushed for him but my new horse had become almost unmanageable from the firing, and ran into a thick bunch of grapevines, and become so badly entangled that he nearly fell with me. I finally got him steadied down when

I saw the old man across the fence with his gun drawn on me. I pulled on him and ordered him to throw down his gun, which he did. I then saw another old man near him, gun in hand, whom I also made surrender. Then farther along, I saw a third, a boy of about sixteen. I made him surrender also. When not seeing any more, I looked back at old man No. 1 and saw that he had his gun up to his face again—I could see his eye over his gun. I saw that talk would no longer go as he had probably discovered that I was alone, so fired at him and threw myself forward on my horse's neck to receive his fire. He did fire and I felt that I was hit, as something like an electric shock passed through me, but I could not tell where I was hurt. I pulled on him again and again made him throw down his gun. I did not attempt to fire again because I was doubtful if I had any more loads in my gun, and had no time to ascertain. I made the men walk away from their guns, then I extricated my horse, which I found had also been hit, as the blood was running down his neck and shoulders. Just then, Bob Collins, who had heard shooting and my orders to them to surrender, came to my rescue. We could hear the other boys going toward the town, raising a great uproar.

Bob helped me to get the prisoners into the road, where I discovered that I had a bullet through my thigh, and it beginning to be painful, I told him to go on and help the boys, and I would return slowly to camp with the prisoners, that they could overtake me when they had an opportunity. I drove the prisoners ahead, but by some mischance we took a wrong road, one branching off to the right, at an angle of perhaps thirty degrees.

I soon overtook an old negro and his wife, who were in a one horse carry-all or democrat wagon, who were trying to escape to the Yankees. He had in the wagon some five or six bags of flour and perhaps fifteen woolen blankets. I learned that he was from a nearby plantation.

By this time my leg had become so sore that I thought I could not ride in a saddle any longer, so I had the old negro set out all the flour except one bag, then make me a bed with the blankets, and leave his wife to return home. I kept the negro for a driver. I let the boy ride by his side, the old man No. 2 ride my horse, and old man No. 1, who had shot me, I made run on ahead. We, then, in this manner, started for our camp some twenty-two miles away. I then laid one of my empty revolvers at my side for instant use, while I recharged the other, then exchanged and recharged the first. I thought my prisoners looked foolish when they saw that I had been guarding them with empty guns.

We had traveled thus for about five miles when our boys overtook us. They had got near the town and found that the wagon guards hadn't stampeded worth a cent, and had returned to the pickets' camp, where they picked up and destroyed twenty-four guns, left by the pickets, then discovered by my tracks that I had taken a wrong road, had followed, and found me at a time when my leg was paining me so badly that I was speculating in my own mind what I should do with my prisoners.

I had felt particularly spiteful toward old man No. 1, because he had shot me, after he had surrendered. I have since changed my mind on the subject. I now think that it is as much the duty of a prisoner of war to kill his captor and escape if he can, as it is to obey an order of his superior officer.

The missile which had hit me was a square piece of lead, cut from a bar, and was fired with others, from a shotgun. It had entered the leg just above the knee, hitting the bone but not breaking it, passing up to and lodging against the skin near the hip. I have it yet as a memento.

The horse was so badly hurt that we soon abandoned him, and some general was robbed of a beautiful and stylish charger. Before the charge, I had about decided to present him to Colonel C. H. De Groat, of my old regiment, who had recommended me for detail as a scout.

When we arrived within two miles of camp, my wound had became exceedingly sore. It was now quite dark and we found a wagon train stuck in the mud of a long red clay hill. As my wagon could proceed no further, I was put on a horse to enable me to pass the train and soon we met a cavalry regiment who was coming past the train, single file. There was just room for them to pass and we stepped our horses aside to let them go by. My sore leg was on the side on which they were passing, and I think every man in the regiment rubbed his knee against mine. I thought it was the longest regiment I ever saw. It seemed to me that there was enough of them to crush the Confederacy without any help.

As all things must end, so did our night march. I was put in a small tent and Dr. Duncan, headquarters surgeon, sent for. He came and cut out the slug and found a piece of my drawers about an inch square which had been carried clear through the leg.[1]

There was at this time a lady and her daughter in camp, occupying the next tent to mine. They were refugees from Columbia. The daughter hearing that a wounded man had been brought in, came in and held the candle, while the surgeon removed the bullet.

I have since learned that she was the beautiful daughter of the noted "Mrs. Feaster." This daughter, having afterward become of worldwide notoriety, was finally beheaded in Japan by order of the Mikado.[2]

34

Face Off with Rebels

Yet after all, after Love, what is more
attractive to the human heart, than war?

THE PROGRESS OF the army was now nearly at a standstill. The right wing, by reason of taking the shorter route, was somewhat in advance of the left wing, and while the right was stuck in the mud of Lynch Creek swamps, the left had also to surmount this same difficulty, but in addition, had considerable trouble crossing the Catawba River.

This was very annoying to the army commander, who had been making every effort to head off Hardee's army, whose retreat from Charleston must necessarily be across our front in its endeavor to join Beauregard, who was trying to concentrate all the forces possible in our front to impede our progress and strike a terrible blow that would, at least temporarily, relieve Lee from the necessity of abandoning Richmond.

It had always been a part of the duty of the scouts to secure information by obtaining newspapers of late date. Recent captures of papers had given evidence that Charleston was on the eve of being abandoned. Negroes who had overheard whisperings from their masters and mistresses had informed us that that city had fallen.[1]

On the day I was wounded, February 22nd, we had received fairly authentic rumors that Charleston was certainly evacuated. Immediately on receiving this news, General Howard ordered the scouts to cut loose from the army and make their way to the railroad leading from that city to Wilmington, at a point near Florence, and there to destroy as many bridges as possible, to prevent the passage of Hardee's army and military supplies to reinforce the enemy in our front.

At daybreak next morning the scouts started, following down the Camden road a few miles, then taking a road leading towards their proposed destination. They had not proceeded far when they came to a swollen stream (probably Big Lynch), where the bridge had been burned, and found no means of crossing same save by swimming their horses. They accordingly plunged in and gained the opposite shore, where they were attacked by a force of the enemy many times their number and were handled rather roughly. Fortunately no one was hit but they were compelled to recross the stream rather hastily, many having lost their hats and a few their horses. They returned to headquarters and reported that they were not strong enough in number to accomplish the task.

There was no cavalry at hand and it being very important that this work should be done quickly, General Howard ordered a portion of his body guard and Signal Corps to reenforce the scouts. Our old chief, Captain Duncan, was placed in command of the expedition, which started again on the morning of the 24th.[2]

They met with no enemy that day and had got well on their way by 4 o'clock P.M. About this time they were passing a house, on the porch of which stood a lady, who they judge by the motion of her hands was counting them. She would raise her hand and bring it down like a man would do in counting a drove of passing sheep. She was thus enabled to report the exact number, which it was later learned she did do, as "52 invading Yankees." It was afterwards learned that a body of the enemy's cavalry had been following this force for several hours watching an opportunity to pounce upon them when least expected. They had sent out couriers to other small bands of Confederates to concentrate and attack our small force and kill or capture them at one blow.

About the time darkness set in, a fine misty rain commenced falling and bid fair to last during the night. This was regarded by the scouts as favorable to their enterprise. When still light enough to see a little, they came to a crossroads. The two left-hand corners were cleared and fenced, the two right-hand ones being covered with timber. Here they found a Rebel picket post with whom they exchanged shots. The pickets retreated down the lane as far as they were pursued, but no farther. They seemed anxious to decoy our men into what the scouts felt was a trap. They were, however, not looking for traps just then.

Captain Duncan ordered a guard placed out on each of the roads and the balance to slip their bridles and feed their horses. Each man was to stand beside his own horse ready to bridle and mount at an instant's warning, and while the horses were eating, to eat a lunch themselves.

Another road intersected the one on which they had come some twenty rods from the corners where the lunch was taken. Pat Wallace, who had been sent to the rear as a picket, passed this road and had gone about twenty rods farther to the rear. Experience had taught the scouts that in case of small parties traveling like this, through the enemy's country, it was always of more importance to watch the rear than the front.

By the time the horses had finished their feed, it had become so dark that one could see nothing except a white object, ten feet away.

Captain Duncan had ordered all to bridle their horses, then gave the order in a loud tone, "Prepare to mount," which was to be the signal for the pickets to come in.

Scarcely had the men more than got one foot in the stirrup than a loud command came from their rear: "There they are. Charge!" and instantly a rush was made by a large force of the enemy. Nothing could be seen but the tramp of feet indicated that they had gained a point about six or eight rods distant, when our boys turned loose on them with Spencer rifles and revolvers. This caused a temporary halt but soon a voice was heard to say, "Now their guns are empty, give them hell!"

It must be remembered that very few breech-loading carbines were in existence and the Confederates had less chance to learn their usefulness than the Federals. The headquarters guard and Signal Corps were armed with Spencers and had an abundance of ammunition.

The charge was again made and again met with a like reception. Again and again did they charge till at last the two forces were intermingled on those four corners. Suddenly all firing ceased and nothing could be heard but the tramping of horses' feet as they moved about. No one on either side felt safe in shooting, for fear of hitting their own men. Objects could be dimly seen moving about and occasionally a whisper could be heard. Once in a while an indiscreet person would call out and immediately a shot would be fired, sometimes followed by a fall or a groan.

The soldiers of both parties had peculiar dialects, or method of pronunciation. A soldier would be able, even in the dark, to recognize in the speech of the "Yankees" that they were enemies, and so on our side, a word spoken aloud and one would instantly be able to distinguish it as emanating from a friend or an enemy. Here was a case where silence was golden.

A white horse was very unpopular that night, for that was the only object that could be traced with any certainty.

It seems that Pat Wallace, who was picketing the rear, heard the advance of the cavalry, which was coming into the main road by the fifth road, before mentioned, between him and our forces. He thought that our forces were leaving without notifying him and started to join them, when he suddenly ran into the Confederate cavalry and asked in a low tone, "What command is this?" "It don't matter, fall in here, we are going to charge them," a voice answered. Pat was wise enough to grasp the situation and did fall in as commanded, but soon took an opportunity to give them the slip. He reported that there was from eight hundred to one thousand of the Confederates.

In the early part of the melee, Lieutenant McQueen, Joe Bedoll, and Dawson recognized each other and agreed in a whisper to remain together. McQueen rode a white horse and he and the two others stood side by side, with McQueen in the center, facing the enemy.

There had been several intervals of silence and there was one that the boys declare lasted a full fifteen minutes, with the road full of men, some moving about, but not a word was spoken.

Near the close of this interval two men, one of whom rode a white horse, gradually approached the group of McQueen and the others. When the horses' heads nearly touched, they came to a halt and each waited for the other to speak. At length McQueen could not bear the suspense and asked, "Who are you?" Instantly the man riding the white horse fired, hitting McQueen in the groin, breaking the pubic bone. He again fired, killing Dawson instantly, and again fired, slightly wounding Bedoll. Joe was a man that could always be counted on to do a soldier's duty. He returned the fire, killing the man on the white horse and wounding the other man. Just then a party of Confederates who stood close by came forward and made Joe a prisoner, taking him to the rear. Again silence prevailed, which lasted so long that the boys each concluding that the other had retreated or been killed, silently stole away, each going in such direction as his judgment dictated. It was afterward learned that the Confederates did the same. It happened that John White and Wallace had got together and they went down the lane a short distance, then let down the fence and rode through, only to find themselves in a boggy swamp. Here they remained till the first break of day, when White crawled back to the scene of the previous night's engagement. He gained the fence which separated him from the road, when looking through between the rails, he saw several dark objects lying on the ground and heard a groan from one near him. He asked in a low tone who it was and learned that it was McQueen, who had lain there all night, unable to move. McQueen said the Rebs had left at the same time the scouts did. By this time two more of the scouts and one of the headquarters guards came up.

On examining the ground they found five Federals and nine Confederates dead, and several Confederates badly wounded, but none of ours except McQueen.

Among others they found the body of the one who had shot McQueen and killed Dawson. He proved to be a Colonel Bailey, of, if I remember correctly, the 2nd South Carolina Cavalry. He had in his pocket a recently signed commission as brigadier general.

By this time it was sufficiently light to see a house a quarter of a mile distant down the lane, where they carried McQueen and left him in care of the occupants. They kindly promised to care for him to the best of their ability. The man of the house was a badly crippled soldier who had served over two years with Lee in Virginia.

Lieutenant McQueen proved to be wounded in the lower abdomen, the pubic bone being crushed, compelling him to this day, as I have been informed, to use crutches.[3]

35

Lieutenant McQueen

Their wishes were neither to live or die,
But to do both alike commendably.

OUR BOYS ARRIVED in camp during the day singly and by twos and threes.

Bedoll, who had been captured, was taken away soon after his capture. His horse was led by a guard, and a guard rode on either side and others followed behind. They kept up a conversation for some time, in which Joe learned that the force attacking was a brigade commanded by General Baily.[1] That Baily had been killed in the action, and many other details. He learned that they knew to a certainty the Federal number and surmised their destination and errand.

The lady who had counted the "sheep" had told them the number. They said they had been following for ten or twelve miles previous to the attack.

Sometime after midnight the rain having increased, the men became sleepy and conversation ceased. Joe then watched his chance, when going over an unusually muddy road, and rolled off his horse into the mud, where he lay until the entire force had passed. Fortunately none of the horses stepped on him.

He then started in the direction he supposed our column lay and traveled mostly in the woods. Sometime in the afternoon of the next day, after having gone about seventeen miles, he discovered that he was going away from our forces and had to retrace his steps.

He arrived at headquarters on the evening of the third day, the hungriest, dirtiest, and most woebegone specimen of humanity I ever saw. He had lost his hat and his clothing was completely covered with mud of the red clay variety.

After my wound, I rode the first day in an ambulance, but the muscles of the thigh were so badly mangled by that square chunk of lead that the motion of the vehicle gave me much pain. The second day I had a bed rigged up on top of our scouts' wagon, and rode much more comfortably. The third day I had a carpenter make me a rude pair of crutches to enable me to get about a little when in camp. The provost guard generally camped near us and I frequently saw the prisoners whom I had taken, one of whom had shot me. By this time I had got over my anger at him and recognized his right and duty as a soldier, to do as he had done. I so stated to him but he did not seem to want to be communicative.

However, as provisions were no great object to the scouts, who always had plenty of them, I saw to it that my prisoners, as I called them, were always well supplied by sending a supply of cooked food by my servant.

Poor old man, I presume he has long since answered his last roll call. Such is a soldier's life. He may have been a good man.

On the fourth day, not being adept at the use of crutches, I had a severe fall, which hurt my leg badly, and I broke one of the crutches around a tree. On the fifth day the same thing happened again, and I broke the remaining crutch. By the use of a cane, I soon became able to walk a little.

I knew that the time was not far distant when dispatches would again be sent to the sea, and as General Sherman had promised me that I should be one of those selected to carry them, I was anxious to be able to ride a horse again because I was convinced that the war would soon close and I would never have another opportunity to distinguish myself.

This may appear to the average reader to be boyish, egotistical, vanity, or what you will, but I want to say here and now, that without that sentiment, or whatever name you wish to give it, no soldier ever amounted to anything. He was simply a cog in the machine, a dolt, a serf. The bombastic crossroads politician may talk about patriotism till your ears ring, but I think the average reader will bear me out in saying that patriotism is for the old men, glory for the boys. Old men are conservative, young men are impetuous. Conservatism never learned anything new, never invented anything, always like the old way the best. Young men are the inventors, the discoverers, the enthusiasts, the soldiers. Imagine an army of old men invading a country. They might be all right in defending a fort or their own fireside, but when it comes to a March to the Sea, or a Sheridan's Ride, it requires men whose blood courses rapidly through their veins. In other words, old men for sense, and young men, for—well, let the reader give it a name.

On the 25th, General Howard authorized the boys to use a flag of truce to visit McQueen, and if he was able to be removed, to bring him in; if not, to leave with him money and medical supplies necessary for his recovery and comfort.

By this time the army had moved up to a point parallel to, and distant about fifteen miles from, where the night fight had taken place.

They found the Rebel pickets about four miles from McQueen. The pickets reported that he was unable to be transported and advised that he be left where he was. They permitted one man to go and see the lieutenant.

As Collins was an old-time, ante-war neighbor and friend of McQueen's, he was selected to go.

Bob found McQueen resting easy and feeling cheerful. A Confederate surgeon had dressed his wound. He had been paroled and the Rebel soldier, at whose house he was staying, was treating him like a brother. It was not known at that time what the probabilities were as to his final recovery. From what Bob could learn, the chances were against him. As Collins was not allowed to remain but one hour, he left with the host the medicine, some sugar and coffee, and about $2,000 in Confederate money, took from McQueen some love and home messages for his family, and left with little hope of ever seeing him again. After the surrender of the Confederate Armies, when our armies were at Washington ready to be mustered out of the service, the boys were surprised and overjoyed to see McQueen come hobbling in on crutches. He had been treated royally by his host and, when able to travel, was assisted to one of our posts, where he was forwarded to Washington.

He is now, I believe, living at McQueen, Illinois, where he is in business and, I presume, one of those pensioners who are robbing the government of some of the money that the poor bondholders, who had saved the country at 25 percent interest, should receive.[2]

36

Longtonen

Nor fire nor brazen wall can keep out fate.

ABOUT FEBRUARY 27th, while I was riding through the mud on top of an army wagon, chafing with impatience to be again in the saddle, the boys were having an experience both amusing and sad.

They had been away, off to the right oblique, and were returning to gain the main road in advance of a moving column, when they discovered two men dressed in blue who were on mules and were trying to get away in the direction of the enemy.

At this stage of the war, it was a very common thing to find the enemy dressed in Federal uniform. Sometimes nearly whole regiments, especially cavalry, were hard to distinguish from our own men. This blue clothing was obtained different ways, sometimes by captures of camps or army wagons, but more often by the stripping of prisoners.

The scouts had become wary of even a blue coat when seen on the back of mounted soldier away from camp. They pursued the two men and overtook them after a two-mile chase. The men had belabored their poor mules to escape from the supposed Rebels, but finally were compelled to give up the race with visions of an Andersonville or a Salisbury in their minds. They proved to be foragers from a Wisconsin Regiment and were exceedingly glad to learn that they were not to be prisoners.

Being now about where the night camp was to be, they decided to advance a little farther toward the front, which they did, accompanied by the foragers. They soon came to a place called "Longtonen," a town of three or four houses or plantations, scattered along the road for a half mile or more.[1]

The boys stopped at the first house, which was at the foot of a gradual rise in the road to the town proper. The foragers went farther up the road and were soon forgotten. The occupants of the house were, as usual, a lady with her grown daughter, who was beautiful and accomplished. It was remarkable what a large number of Southern families there were who had beautiful grown daughters.

At this place there was a fine lawn of Bermuda grass in front of the house, and Amick, who was now Acting Chief of Scouts, got permission of the madam for the horses to graze in the yard. The horses were allowed to roam at will, being confined only by the yard fence. Bedoll, White, and Wallace remained outside as a sort of guard or picket, while the balance were in the parlor listening to the "Bonny Blue Flag" and similar pieces, as rendered by the young lady on her piano.

This lasted perhaps an hour, when suddenly a great racket was kicked up on the hill toward the town. On looking toward the town, they discovered the two foragers coming down on their mules, with kettles, pans, chickens, hams and other things, and perhaps fifty Rebs (mounted), after them. The Rebs succeeded in capturing one of the foragers, but the other one, having perhaps a faster mule, came down towards the boys, closely followed by two of the Confederates. The balance seeing our boys come pouring out of the house and a number of saddled horses in the yard, hesitated, apparently fearing a trap or ambush. Bedoll and Wallace quickly mounted their horses, and Bedoll opened the gate and stood at its front to rescue the forager and to give the boys an opportunity to escape. The forager rushed his mule in through the gate and threw himself off at Joe's feet and looked pleadingly up into this face for protection. He was followed by one of the Rebels, the other remaining outside the gate awaiting events. They evidently thought our boys were their partisans. The one inside demanded of the forager that he surrender, at the same time holding a revolver down on him. The forager would look first at the Rebel, then at Joe, and was speechless. The Rebel kept demanding his surrender and said to Joe, "He is my prisoner." Joe, who was at his side and a little to his rear, demanded of Mr. Reb that he surrender. The Confederate paid no attention to Joe but said to the forager, "Surrender or I'll kill you," at the same time shoving his gun to within a foot of his head. Joe, who had already made two or three demands on him to surrender, saw that to save the forager's life, he must shoot and very quickly fired and the man tumbled off his horse. This shot told the story to the Confederates on the hill, forty rods distant, that it was Yankees they had to deal with, and they charged accordingly. In the meantime Wallace had moved to the upper end of the yard and opened a side gate, and rode into the road between the man outside the front gate and his friends. Seeing his retreat cut off, the Reb started down the road toward our column, with Wallace in close pursuit. It was comical to see a Yankee in grey clothing chasing a Reb in blue clothing. This pursuit continued for nearly a mile, when they ran into our infantry advance guard, which opened ranks and let the blue Rebel pass through, then closed ranks and held up Wallace, the grey Yankee. Wallace, in his excitement, tried to tell them that the other fellow was a Reb, but they only laughed at him. So the blue Reb passed on and rode into the swamp and escaped. Pat frothed at the mouth and fairly danced at what he called the stupidity of the advance guard and could not for some time see that the laugh was on him.

But to return to the other boys: They had at the first alarm rushed out of the house and tried to catch their horses. All but two, Amick and another, succeeded, but they had considerable trouble in doing so. Then they had to bridle them. This took time and the Rebels were coming down the road on the run. Those who were ready would not desert the balance and waited to fight it out if necessary, and to survive or perish together. This is the kind of nerve it takes to make a scout.

At length the boys got their horses, but in the meantime the cavalry got down so near that it was not safe to try to escape through the front gate, so they passed out of a rear gate and through a garden into the woods beyond. The next day the scouts returned to the house and learned that the Rebels had made a hasty retreat after the events spoken of, probably by reason of the arrival of our advance guard. The ladies had taken the wounded man into the house and one of our surgeons had dressed his wound. The ball had passed entirely through his head just behind the eyes. Both eyes were destroyed. They had talked with him about the scrap. He said he had heard Joe demanding his surrender, but thought he was talking to the forager. He admitted it was a mistake and did not blame Bedoll. The boys left with him such things as would add to his comfort and passed on.

In 1866, I was crossing the harbor of Charleston on a ferry boat when I noticed a man with blue glasses on, who was pointing out to his little son the different points of interest to be seen. I saw that he frequently pointed in a wrong direction so concluded that he was blind. Curiosity prompted me to question him as to how he had lost his sight. He said that a Yankee bullet had deprived him of his sight. I asked him where it had occurred and he replied at a place called "Longtonen." I then knew that he was the man whom Bedoll had shot. As I exhibited considerable interest and curiosity in the event, he gave me the particulars, which did not differ materially from the report of the scouts.

Bedoll was at that time in command of the City Prison at Charleston and I was on my way to visit him. I asked the man if he would like to become acquainted with the man who had shot him and he answered that he would. That he held no ill feelings against him—that it was simply a legitimate event of the war and no one was personally to blame.

I took his address and told Joe of the circumstance and asked him to go with me to see the man. Joe could not make up his mind to go. I think he felt as bad over it as if the man had been his brother.

37

Recovered

But now the Powers of Beauty, Song and Wine,
Which are most men's delight, are also mine.

I HAD BEEN practicing, trying to exercise the muscles of my leg to enable
me to ride, when the time came to ride to the sea with dispatches. I had
saved up a very fine, easy riding mare that I had secured back south of the
Edisto for just this purpose.

By reason of my not being able to get about at Cheraw, I did not see
much of that city.[1]

After crossing the Pedee [Pee Dee] at Cheraw, headquarters moved
out ten or twelve miles and went into camp. The next day, being the tenth
day of my wound, I tried riding a little and found I could endure it by being careful. The eleventh day I rode with the boys to show them I could.
We had an easy ride until two or three o'clock in the afternoon, when we
suddenly came into a small town, called Laurenburg [Laurinburg], North
Carolina, where, much to our surprise, we found a railroad and two loco-
motives and several cars. One engine had steam up but the railroad men
had disappeared.

We destroyed the outfit, and my leg by that time had become quite sore,
so I stayed at the depot till the boys ran over town. They soon returned and
White was greatly excited, telling me in a whisper that he had been poi-
soned. That he had drank something the boys had got, that made his throat
feel like he had a splinter in it, and had temporarily lost his voice. They had
brought some of the poison with them and I sampled it and pronounced it
the finest quality of very old peach brandy. I then sampled it some more to
make sure that it was not poison, and soon decided that it was not safe for

White to be carrying so much poison with him and took charge of it myself for future reference.

It then began to rain and we remembered that camp was to be at Laurel Hill, two miles away. We rode rapidly to that place and found it a country post office and that the army had not yet arrived.

While talking with the negroes there, we learned that three Rebels had left there but a few minutes before our arrival. By this time White's poison had made us forget all about the rain, and I about my sore leg, and we decided to pursue and capture the Rebs. We rode two or three miles before coming in sight of them. It was beginning to get dark, and instead of slipping up on them as we should have done, one of the boys fired and of course they scattered in a hurry. One of them turned into a byroad, and I, seeing he had a very fine horse, and I having as good a one, followed him while the other boys followed the other men. My horse proved the faster one and my Reb left the road and tried to escape me by dodging through the bushes.

By this time I did not know I had a sore leg. In the race I lost my hat and would probably have lost my man, had not his horse stumbled and fell, rolling the man some distance. I soon got to him, dismounted, and helped him up. No bones were broken but he was badly shaken up, and it was some time before he was able to ride. He proved to be an old man of considerable importance. He had worn a large, old-fashioned, white, long-furred high hat. It lay on the ground, and I, thoughtlessly, put it on my head. Of course, I knew at once that he was not a soldier, but regarding him as some high civil dignitary, informed him he must go to camp with me. He acquiesced and I, not being able to put him on his large cream stallion, helped him on to my horse while I rode his.

I did not see the boys again till I got to camp. I had become completely soaked with the rain, and when we got back to Laurel Hill, I found the army there. Headquarters were near at hand, and I thought to take my prisoner directly to General Howard instead of turning him over to the Provost Guard, the usual way. The rain had ceased and I found that a string band was serenading the general. The musicians were sitting on camp stools on my side of the fires in a row, while a dozen or more officers, including General Howard, were standing on the opposite side, facing me. As I came within the light of the fires, I saw Colonel Conklin, A.Q.M. for the Army of the Tennessee, coming rapidly toward me. I knew at once that I was doing something wrong and halted, awaiting the colonel. White's poison had prevented me from realizing the absurdity of a soldier making his appearance before the general with a white plug hat on, and General Howard at that.

Colonel Conklin had grasped the situation at once and advanced to save me the humiliation and censure that must necessarily follow my advent before the general.

I said to him, "Colonel, I have a gentleman here, who I think the general would like to interview." He replied, "Very well, I will take charge of him." The gentleman dismounted, handed me the bridle, and started, but soon turned to look at me and I saw at once what the trouble was. It was the first time I had noticed that he was quite old and very baldheaded. Then I remembered that I had his hat. I said to him, "I beg your pardon, sir, I will return your hat. I would not have asked you for it but I have been recently wounded, and did not want to take a cold." He replied, "You was welcome, sir." And that was the way I got out of that scrape.

From 1880 to 1890, Colonel Conklin was a neighbor of mine in Nebraska. He remembered the occurrence distinctly and always spoke of me as "The white hatted scout."

After delivering my prisoner to Colonel Conklin, I went to the scouts' quarters, where I found the boys. After my supper, Amick came to me and said that General Sherman had sent for him and Collins and informed them that they were to start for Wilmington before daylight next morning. I asked why I was not to go. He said he did not know. I immediately called my servant and sent for my horse to ride down to General Sherman's tent, some two hundred yards away. I instructed my servant to station himself as near the general's tent as I would be allowed to ride, and there to wait for me, to hold my horse.

When I arrived at the general's tent, I found the flap open and a good light within and a bright fire in front. The general was writing at a table facing the door. I left my horse with my servant and walked without a cane or a limp toward him, saluted, and said: "General, down at Savannah I understood you to say that I should be the one who would be called to make this expedition to Wilmington." He said, "Well, yes, but let me see. Oh, yes. They told me you were wounded and could not go." I answered, "Yes, General, but it was only a scratch and is well now, and I would like to go." He said, "All right, you shall go." I thanked him, saluted, and retired. I was sorry to deprive Collins of the "Glory," but thought I was entitled to it.

38

Notes from General Howard

Victory is noble, how much more
To do as never Greek before.

THE NEXT MORNING, which was March 8th, at three o'clock, we were up and ready for a start and called at General Sherman's tent. He was up with pantaloons on, and suspenders hanging down and slippers on his feet, rummaging through some papers apparently in a nervous state. His hair stood every way for Sunday. He could not find the thing he was looking for and sent an orderly for Adjutant General Dalton, who was in the next tent, who came in and brought our dispatch and duplicate. They were written on a piece of tissue paper about the size of a greenback, but not cut so squarely. They looked as though they had been torn haphazard from a large sheet and were written in the code cipher and looked like a small scrap on which a schoolboy had been practicing making letters and words.

The general explained to us the contents so that in the event of our being compelled to destroy them, and afterward succeeding in getting through to Wilmington, we could relate to General Terry[1] or whoever was in command, what was wanted.

Translated it read as follows:

Headquarters Military Division of the Mississippi.

In the Field, Laurel Hill, Wed., Mch. 8, 1895. We are marching for Fayetteville, will be there Saturday, Sunday or Monday, and will then March for Goldsboro.

If possible send a boat up Cape Fear River and have word conveyed to General Schofield that I expect to meet him about Goldsboro. We are all well and have done finely. The rains make our roads difficult and may delay us about Fayetteville, in which case I would like to have some bread, sugar and coffee. We have abundance of all else. I expect to reach Goldsboro by the 20th inst.

W.T. Sherman,
Major General
[This episode is covered in Sherman's *Memoirs*, Chapter XXIII, pages 775–76.][2]

Not having delivered my copy of the dispatch at Wilmington, I kept it for several years, and at one time could have repeated it from memory. Now, however, I can only remember the first four words. As that cipher code has long since gone out of use and been superseded by a newer and better one, I will here say that it began without system, method, or order. The words remembered are "Cairo, fight, bill Kitchen." There were not half as many words as in the translation and it contained no punctuation or capitals.

On handing them to us, the general said, "Now, boys, I am going to send a regiment of cavalry with you as far as Lumberton to drive out a Rebel company of cavalry who are there. Then you will make your way from there in your own way. I have learned that this company belongs to a regiment whose headquarters are at Elizabeth (Elizabethtown), where I presume they will retreat to. You must look out for them. I think you had better make your way to a point near Elizabeth, then turn off and get to the river, turn your horses loose, capture a skiff or canoe, and float down to Wilmington."

We did not like this plan and I said to him: "General, if you so order it, we will do so, but if you will leave it to our own discretion, we will stick to our horses. You know that down on the Ogeechee we went hunting gunboats by water and got heartily tired of it." He answered, "Well, use your own judgment, but that in my opinion is the best and safest plan. I sent Corporal Pike last night with this same dispatch and he will take to the river route." As we were leaving, he said, "Now, remember boys, the first one who gets there gets the reward." I said to him, "General, that does not look to me as being fair, for you have given Pike several hours the start of us." He answered, "Oh, well, I guess you will be able to make it."[3]

This was rather discouraging to us, but we were in it now and concluded to make an extreme effort to get there first.

The reader must remember that it was not known to a certainty that Wilmington was in our possession, but it was so rumored and believed to be true. In the event of it not being in our hands, we were to exercise our best judgment in getting to the mouth of Cape Fear River, where our friends and the fleet would surely be.

In an article from the pen of Major General O. O. Howard published in the *National Tribune* of March 12, 1896, referring to some of the closing events of the great Carolina Campaign, he says:

> General Sherman very much desired to get communications to Wilmington and if possible receive back word from the same, while Logan and I were anxious to re-establish mail communications. After consulting with Captain Duncan, I selecting Sergeant Myron J. Amick, 15th Ill. Cavalry, and Sergeant George W. Quimby, 32nd Wisconsin, the two enlisted men who it will be remembered had made the perilous and successful expedition down the Ogeechee near Savannah, through the enemy's lines and communicated with the fleet; these furnished with as much mail matter as well as dispatches as they could comfortably carry, I started off for Wilmington.
>
> Sherman had sent another messenger to float down the Cape Fear. My party crossed the river at Campbell's Bridge and succeeded in avoiding or deceiving squads of the enemy's cavalry, or other hostiles whom they met, and finished their journey successfully in forty-eight hours. Just after our arrival at Fayetteville and after the first excitement of the skirmishing had subsided, we heard the whistle of a steam tug below us on the Cape Fear River. This vessel had set out at once for Fayetteville on receiving news through Sergeants Amick and Quimby of our whereabouts.[4]

In April 1894, I received a letter from General Howard, of which the following is an extract:

> Headquarters Dept. of the East,
> Governors Island, N.Y.
> April 14, 1894
> Capt. George Quimby,
> Verdigre, Nebraska.

My dear Sir:

I remember with great distinctness your expedition down the Ogeechee with Amick and Captain Duncan. Admiral Dahlgren mentions you in his Washington Dispatches and my brother, General C.H. Howard, lately wrote an article for the Loyal Legion in Chicago giving a history of your daring and successful exploits.[5] I also remember that you bore dispatches from General Sherman and myself across the Carolinas when it was dangerous to do so, carrying them to General Terry, then supposed to be at Wilmington, N.C. You were made Captain, I think, as a recognition of your daring.

Hoping that this may find you well, I remain,
Very truly yours,
(Signed) O.O. Howard
Major General U.S. Army

The following is from the Knox County (Nebraska) *Recorder*, published by E. H. Purcell, at Verdigre, Nebraska, in April 1894: "In a series of articles which have from time to time appeared in the *National Tribune*, from the pen of Maj. Gen. O.O. Howard, our townsman, Capt. Geo. W. Quimby has repeatedly received special mention in his capacity as scout, in some of the most daring and successful exploits which occurred during the Civil War. He was young, reckless, and although captured numerous times while working inside the Confederate lines, always managed to escape. Great confidence seems to have been placed in him by his Superior officers, for his ability to deliver dispatches of importance, under the gravest dangers."

39

Dispatches to General Terry

Porcius and Marphadates, friends so true
One soul, they say, suffices for the two.

A SMALL REGIMENT of cavalry being in waiting, we started off on the road toward Lumberton, twenty miles to the south, Amick and I riding in the rear, where we could discuss the situation. We did not like the plans laid out for us. The fact that this Confederate company was to be driven out and forced on to the road ahead of us, the very road we were to take, would place them in our front and necessarily impede our progress, if not effect our capture. We had learned that the road from Lumberton, which we were to take, was at a right angle to the one we were on, and reasoned that if we were to cut off that angle by taking a diagonal road to the left and travel rapidly, we could place ourselves between that company and Elizabethtown, and would not have them to contend with. We then began to look for such a diagonal road, and when it had become daylight and we were yet about eight miles from Lumberton, we saw such a one.

There was a house nearby, before which stood an old man about six-and-half-feet tall. We, that is Amick and I, halted to inquire of him about the roads. From his description this was the one we wanted, as he stated that it intersected the Lumberton and Elizabethtown road about eight miles from the former place.

I shall always remember this man for the following reasons: he had no nose and spoke very indistinctly. I asked him his name but could not understand his answer and asked him to spell it. He said "RO zed IER." I then remembered that my grandfather had told me that the Z was pronounced Zed in his boyhood days.

We made good time across this road, and shortly before we gained the other road, we heard musketry in the direction of Lumberton. We congratulated ourselves on being in advance of the Rebel company and hastened on toward Elizabethtown, some sixty miles away with no town between it and us.

Another rain set in, which lasted fully thirty hours. It was a very dismal lonely ride. I had a rubber poncho which protected me from the rain down to my legs, which soon became thoroughly soaked. This and my previous day's ride soon began to tell on my wounded leg and I became so sore and stiff, that I could not dismount without help.

We then saw the folly of my undertaking this trip, but it was now too late to substitute another man. We rode all day without a rest or feed, fearing that the Rebel forces in our rear would overtake us. After dark we became very hungry and our horses showed unmistakably evidences of needing rest and food. Then we began looking for a safe place to stop and refresh ourselves and horses. About 9 o'clock P.M. we came to a plantation where the houses were near the road, and saw a lane leading down a row of negro quarters, which we followed quietly to try to find some negroes who would help us out. After passing a dozen of the houses that were without a light or sound, we came to one from which we could hear a banjo and the shuffling of feet, but no other noises. I held Amick's horse while he reconnoitered to see if any white people were about. This was necessary at that time because the masters were very suspicious of the negroes, especially, when the Yankee Army was known to be near or approaching, and it was not unusual for the master or overseer to snoop around at all hours at night to see that all was quiet and no conspiracies were being hatched by the blacks.

Amick had first to reconnoiter outside and then wait for one of the negroes to come out where he could interview him. In about half an hour Amick returned with an old black man, who took us some distance further down the lane, where I was helped into a house, where an old mammy prepared for us a good supper of baked sweet potatoes, corn pone, and bacon. Amick sent other negroes out as a picket on the main road to see if any of the Confederates should pass. We were especially worried about the company in our rear. We knew that if they became aware of the fact that Yankees were ahead of them, they would surmise the object of their trip and make every effort for our capture. While we were waiting for our supper, Amick placed his copy of the dispatches closely folded in one corner of a huge plug of navy tobacco, intending in case of capture, to take a chew from the particular corner and then offer a chew to his captor. As I did not chew tobacco, I could not resort to that scheme, but had to think of another equally safe.

I drew one of the bullets from my right-hand revolver and cut off a portion of its butt end, then placed my copy in against the powder and put the bullet back to place. I then revolved the cylinder so that this charge would be the last one to be fired. I reckoned that if I had occasion to use the revolver, that dispatch would never meet the eyes of a Rebel soldier. Again if I should be captured without having first fired the weapon, whoever got it would sooner or later fire it off, which would be the last of my dispatches.

We here learned that we were about twenty miles from Elizabeth. I want to say here that this town was known by the people of the surrounding country as "Elizabeth," while the maps all show it as "Elizabethtown."

The negroes told us that at Elizabeth there were two Rebel companies who did patrol duty on all the principal roads by sending a detail that would travel twenty to thirty miles out one day and back the next, when they would be relieved by another detail.

One of the blacks had lived at Elizabeth and was familiar with the roads. We particularly inquired of him if we could not pass the town by leaving it at one side. He said not, that the plantation fences would throw us off our route and we would miss the right road. He described the road we were to take after getting through the town in quite an intelligent manner, a thing that few negroes in the South could do.

After resting our horses for about two hours, we again started, the rain still continuing to fall. Our picket had reported that no one had passed, so we felt confident that news of our coming had not gone ahead of us.

When we thought we were near the town, Amick reconnoitered some negro houses and brought out a negro who would tell us nothing. He was the first and only black man we had ever found in the South who would not do all in his power to help a Yankee. This one probably took us for home guards who were spying upon him and trying to pass themselves as Yankees. This was a common trick of theirs and many a black man got a severe whipping for being thus caught.

I was very angry at what I thought was his obstinacy and think but for Amick I would have hit him over the head with my revolver. Subsequent events convinced me that as soon as we were gone, he went to his master's house and reported us, and he in turn sent word to the forces in town.

We were nearer to the town than we supposed and, plodding along through the darkness and rain, found ourselves immediately in front of a row of tents near the road we were on. A dim fire was burning near one of them, where probably the usual guard was being sheltered from the rain. At any rate we got through the town without being challenged and soon found the road as we supposed, that the negro had told us to take. We felt now that we were beyond all forces of the enemy and began favoring our horses.

Daylight found us about ten miles from town. Imagine our surprise, chagrin, and disappointment to learn that we had taken the wrong road from town and that, do what we would, even by cutting across the country, we had lost at least ten miles of travel. We had to retrace our steps a couple of miles, then take a diagonal road to the proper one.

We had then traveled one hundred miles with only two hours' rest and our horses were getting very tired.

40

Delayed

The first thing for a Captain is to gain
Safe Victory; the next to be with honor slain.

AFTER GAINING the right road, we soon came to a house that had apparently been built for a public tavern. Here we stopped to see if we could get an exchange of horses. We rode into a wagon yard through a gate. These gates in the South were so arranged that a man on horseback could open them. By the settling of a post, this one was hard to open, and when we were inside, it slammed shut with some force. We had seen a horse in a back lot and asked a lady who came to the side door to exchange with us until we could return. We told her our business was important, that we bore orders from General Beauregard to collect all the scattered detachments to resist the Yankees, who were coming. She replied in substance that we could not have her horse, that "She had got about enough of the Confederacy, anyhow." An old negro mammy had come out to listen and I asked her if she had any victuals cooked. She replied that she had and started to the kitchen to get it for Amick, who had dismounted, when I looked back over the gate and here came a Rebel officer and soldier, mounted. I told Amick to mount quickly and I rushed my horse to the gate, the officer doing the same. I got there first and my horse being very tired and clumsy partly fell against the gate and forced it open. Of course, I had my gun in my hand and my first thought was to shoot him, then I feared that the sound of a shot would bring others to his rescue. His right hand was down behind his leg so I could not see whether he had a gun in it or not, and he had an old-fashioned horse pistol in his belt. Amick had taken the precaution to rush to the other man to see that he did not draw his musket. It instantly occurred to both Amick and myself that the negro had given us away and that a squad of men had followed us to effect our capture and that this officer and man had simply ridden on ahead to see whatever was to be seen.

The captain, for such he proved to be, demanded, "Who are you?" He wore a new dress coat that was of a color between a grey and a blue and at a glance might have been taken for a faded Federal coat. Instead of answering his question, I said to Amick, "He is a Yankee." The captain laughed and said I was mistaken, and in turn asked me where we belonged. I intimated that I did not care to be interrogated by a Yankee. I noticed that he kept looking back down the road from whence he came and felt sure that he was expecting help. I am quite certain that if we had had fresh horses, we would have killed both of them and cut out for Wilmington.

We had before us a half mile of fenced road to travel before we could reach the woods. Once we were there, we felt that we stood a good chance to escape, even if our horses were badly jaded. I was satisfied that we had but a few minutes at most to act. We could easily handle these two men but it was their supporters that we feared. The captain asked me where we were going, and I told him, "Down the road a piece." "Wait a minute," said he, "till I speak to this gentleman," referring to an old man who had come out onto the front gallery. I said, "We will ride along slowly and you can overtake us." Amick and I then started on, but took pains to sit cross-legged looking backwards so they could not get the drop on us. They remained in the road looking first at us, then in the rear, and the captain did not seem to want to speak with the man on the porch.

It would perhaps have been the next thing to an impossibility for us to have spurred our horses into a trot. They had then made fully one hundred miles in thirty hours with but one feed and scarcely any rest. Amick's horse was standing it some better than mine, Amick weighing about one hundred thirty pounds and I nearly fifty pounds heavier.

We had another danger now before us. We had learned at this tavern that each second day, five men would ride down this road about twenty miles and return the next, that they had gone down the previous day and would return this day. This made us still more anxious to get to the end of the fence and into the woods. We had but just got to the corner when we saw the five men coming in our front; they were bundled up to protect themselves from the rain, and while they could see us, they probably did not suspect our identity. At the same time, we saw the captain frantically waving his hat to some men in his rear whom we could not see, and then come rushing after us. We then passed into the woods and out of sight.

Had it not been for my sore leg, we felt that we would now be able to cope with their combined force. I then told Amick if worst came to worst, he must cut out and leave me and get to Wilmington alone. That I had been a prisoner four times and had escaped each time and thought I could do it again, and that I would throw them off his track. His answer was, "What do you take me for?"

The road we had just left was one that had probably been made by the state, as it was laid out straight, the timber cut off and removed for four rods in width, and all the low places graded and streams well bridged, a condition we seldom found in the South. It was the direct road from Elizabeth to Wilmington. We soon came to what had been the old zigzag road between the same places, which had been abandoned when the new one was built. We reckoned that the enemy would try to follow us through the woods and lost no time in getting along the road. We also hoped that they were not aware of the jaded condition of our horses and would give up the chase soon.

41

A Rest

These shields with purple, gold and ivory wrought
Were won by us that but with poor ones fought.

OUR EXPEDITION now assumed a different phase. The enemy were now aware of our presence and probably had surmised our destination and errand. Had they been old and experienced soldiers, our chances of getting to Wilmington would have been small. At the same time if we had had fresh horses and my leg had been well, we felt that we could have bid them defiance. True, it was to be a stern chase, but a steamer with a broken wheel could not have much chance with one with perfect machinery.

Our hope now, however, rested on the supposition that our pursuers were inexperienced home guards and that we might accomplish by maneuvering what we lacked in speed.

After going five or six miles, mostly in the woods, we ventured out to the new road. When we got to it, I tried to have my horse step out just far enough to enable me to see if anyone was in sight, but he was so tired that in trying to step over a small ditch, stumbled along and landed in the middle of the road, where on looking to our front, I saw the same five men going our way, some thirty rods ahead of us, of course with their backs to us so they did not see me. No one was in sight in our rear so we got back into the woods and again found the old road which we traveled and soon came to a considerable stream that in low water was easily fordable, but now from the heavy rains, was a torrent. We reckoned that the five men had gone down to the bridge which spanned this stream on the new road, where they would watch for us. There was now nothing for us, but to take chances in swimming our horses. It was a fearful undertaking but we succeeded in getting across. I would rather have had half a dozen shots fired at me at twenty rods than to have had to cross that stream in the condition myself and horse were in. A few miles further on, we came in sight of a house, the first we had seen since the tavern, and concluded to try to get a feed for our horses and something for ourselves to eat, but on nearing the place, we saw eight or ten saddled horses tied near the front. It is needless to say that we gave that house a wide berth. Within three or four miles as near as I can remember, we came plumb onto a railroad, a thing we were not looking for as our map did not show it. On the opposite side we could see a house, forty rods away, and concluded to try again for something to eat and a feed. Just as I, who was ahead, got onto the track, I saw again our five men standing on the track a quarter of a mile toward Wilmington. I spoke quickly to Amick to pass on and not appear to notice them. When we were out of their sight, we halted and I said to Amick, "It now occurs to me that those men who were at the crossing of the new road, on seeing us and thinking we did not see them, will pass on to a road that will necessarily lead from this house to the main road, and that they would gain that road and follow up to the house and expect to bag us. Now, let us follow the railroad to a point where we just saw them, then follow their tracks carefully, to see if sure enough, they did so, and if they pursued that course we would be between them and our destination."

He agreed to this plan and we found it just as I had anticipated. When we came to where the planter's road intersected ours, we saw their fresh tracks going toward the planter's house as I had predicted. We were now sure that there was no enemy ahead of us, and hoped that these men would give up the chase.

We soon came to a single house, that of one of the poor whites. Here we were determined to have something to eat, and get some information. Just before getting to it, we saw a man enter hastily and shut the door, we called to him, but it was some time before we got an answer, when finally a voice told us to go away or he would kill us. We told him we wished him no harm, but only wanted to talk to him. He said, "I know what you want, you want my son and you can't have him. Now that the Yankees have come, you are going to leave us and you want to take my son to Virginia to fight, and I tell you, you can't have him, I'll kill you if you try to come in." We saw that he took us for conscript officers and it took some time to convince him that we were Yankees and only wanted information as to the roads. He said that a bridge over a stream in our front had been destroyed and that we could not cross there, but by going two miles up we would find a home-made bridge that could not go out. That now it was probably two feet under water, but that it was perfectly safe. He described it so accurately that although it was dark when we got there, we found it as directed, but I want to say that it took more courage than I usually possess to plunge in an unknown body of water to find a bridge, belly deep to a horse, and that too, me with a leg that a Rebel bullet had recently passed through.

We got over safely and soon got back to the main road, where we found a fine plantation house, where we stopped and were informed by the planter that we were now safe—that Wilmington was now in our hands, that he had been there that day and taken the oath of allegiance.[1] He said it was twenty miles to town and that we had better rest and feed our horses till about midnight when we could reach our pickets at daybreak.

This was joyful news to us. I had fallen asleep several times on my horse and really believe I could never have got through but for Amick bracing me up, besides my leg long since had become so bad, that I was in excruciating agony, besides being so hungry. I never possessed much fortitude to endure hunger. Our horses, too, could scarcely move faster than an ox team.

I was helped into the house, where a young lady prepared a pallet on the floor near the fire, where I think I must have fallen asleep inside of one minute. In the course of an hour I was awakened to eat a hearty supper, but as I could not get up, it was brought to me.

Amick had seen to the care of our horses and had a negro at each horse rubbing him down. He also made assurance double sure by stationing negroes out as pickets.

After supper Amick lay down for a short nap, but the young lady would not let me sleep. She was particularly interested in our experience at the tavern and made me describe the Rebel captain several times. At length she said, "Well, but haven't I got a good joke on him. Do you know, sir, that captain is my sweetheart? He has been in the service in the home guards, right around here during the entire war, and has often expressed a wish that he could meet an armed Yankee. Won't I give it to him when I see him?!"

I told how near I came to killing him and I thought she turned pale.

No people could have treated us more kindly than they did, and when we left, they would not accept any remuneration.

At midnight we were given another supper, our horses were saddled and brought around, I was helped into the saddle, and after their expressing a hearty wish for our welfare and the speedy return of peace, we bid them adieu and once more took up our journey to help out "Uncle Billy" and the boys.

42

Dispatches Delivered

Filling evermore his purse, and at the Isthmus gave a treat
To be laughed at, of cold meat.

IT WAS A LONG, slow, tedious, and sleepy ride, but just at early daylight we came in sight of our pickets, two miles from the river, and here, we at once knew without being told, that we had come into an entirely different army than the Western. Here, it was all discipline and red tape.[1] The vidette halted us at long range and made us wait an unnecessary length of time for the reserves to form and march out under a sergeant, who went through with all the formality of a division inspection. The vidette could plainly see that there were but two of us and no place or opportunity for a surprise, but we were delayed fully twenty minutes. Had it been the Western Army and two supposed Rebs were seen coming under this circumstance and surroundings, the vidette would simply have privately notified the reserve and permitted us to walk into their trap.

After notifying the sergeant who we were and our errand, he would not believe us until Amick showed him a pass from General Sherman. Even then he did not grasp the importance of haste and wanted us to remain with them to get breakfast, then march in with them after the relief came at nine o'clock. He said this was orders. We had to storm, scold, and threaten before he would consent to take us in as far as his regiment, which was a half mile in the rear. It seemed that pickets were detailed by company or regiment, which moved out to a point near the picket line with their tents and all their belongings.

When we arrived at their colonel's tent, he was found in a comfortable bed in a large cozy wall tent, a guard in front, etc. The sergeant woke him up and made known his "important capture," and that we claimed to be couriers from General Sherman and wanted to be sent to General Terry at once. The colonel rolled over in bed, and said, "Take them to the guard house—they can be taken in at nine o'clock when the relief arrives."

Now, I have always been impatient of red tape and army discipline and broke out in one of my fits of anger, which, if I had not scared the colonel a little, I think would have made him order us in irons. I said, "Colonel, if you don't immediately send us to General Terry, I'll raise such a smoke around your ears, that you won't forget it in a hurry, this is a matter of great importance. General Sherman wants these dispatches placed in General Terry's hands at *the earliest possible moment!*" He said, "Very well, give them to me and I will send them in." I said, "No sir, they don't leave our hands until they go into General Terry's." He then raised up and came to the front of his tent in his drawers and night shirt. Think of a soldier in the field in a night shirt, and on the picket line at that. It makes me think of Jeff Davis in his wife's shawl.[2] He then told the sergeant to conduct us to General Terry. We soon arrived at the river, where we were ferried over the main stream to the city, where we arrived at General Terry's office at exactly 8 o'clock A.M., having been fifty-three hours on the road, and traveling one hundred forty-four miles.

General Terry had just come into his office when Amick handed him his copy of the dispatch (mine was more difficult to get at). He politely asked us to be seated. I told him I wanted to see a surgeon at once to dress my wound, and he called for his headquarters surgeon, who dressed it for me. My leg was badly swollen and smelled horrible. It had been wet, cold, and irritated for two days.

General Terry then told us to make ourselves comfortable, etc. I told him we were hungry and our horses were nearly dead and needed care. He then sent an orderly for his chief quartermaster, who proved to be General Dodge, A.Q.M. General Terry said to him, "General Dodge, you will issue rations to these men and forage for their horses." Now, had it been in a Western Army, the general would have said to his orderly, "Take these men around to the mess and see that they are well provided for," but here all was different. Dignity and Discipline must be preserved!

Amick was never so bold to shoot off his mouth, as the boys use to say, as I was, and I thanked General Terry and said, "We will provide for ourselves at a hotel, if one is to be found." General Dodge kindly asked us if we had any money or needed any, and was told that we had plenty. General Dodge afterward intimated that he was not pleased with our cold reception by General Terry.

Amick took me to a hotel and our horses to a stable, where he employed a negro to work on them for a whole day. After a breakfast Amick went again to headquarters, where they had succeeded in deciphering the message. You see, General Terry could not take the verbal message from an enlisted man. That would not be "Military," you know, but spent an hour and a half in deciphering the dispatch, then hastily wrote an answering dispatch and sent it by the first gunboat at hand. Not a pound of coffee or sugar or a pair of shoes, as had been requested by General Sherman. Didn't have them to spare, you know. I'll venture to say that there were five shiploads within the sound of a cannon.

General Terry was a very nice gentleman, and all that, but he was educated in the wrong school to be popular with us Western "mud sills."

Amick went down with the dispatch bearer to the gunboat to send some messages to our friends, and the gunboat in its haste went off and took him along. He afterward reported that they met Corporal Pike forty miles up the river in a canoe, with his copy of the dispatch.

I was now alone and had plenty of money and some cheek, and decided that I needed to rest till my wound was improved. I was soon surrounded by reporters for Northern newspapers, who pumped me dry of the particulars of the great march and of our own personal experiences on this trip. All of these were published at the time and created another sensation and excitement at the North.[3] The correspondent of the New York *Herald* had taken possession of a newspaper outfit in the city and was publishing a paper under the name of the Wilmington *Herald*. He wanted to buy our horses with which to distribute papers at the different camps. The Confederates had taken away all horses and the army had brought only half enough of their own use. He told me he could not, by reason of a general order, purchase the horses unless I obtained a special permit from General Dodge to sell them. I asked General Dodge for the permit and he inquired if we owned them. I told him that we did and "Uncle Sam did not own a horse in Sherman's army." He smiled and gave me the permit, and the *Herald* man gave me two hundred dollars for the horses, saddles, and bridles. I was sorry to part with Amick's saddle, as it was a Mexican, and worth sixty-five dollars. The horses could easily be replaced but the saddle could not.

I now considered myself a free moral agent, to go and come as I liked until such time as my leg got well. General Dodge told me that in my present condition there would be no use to try to join the army until it arrived in Goldsboro, when I could do so by ship and railroad. Steamers were daily going to and from Fortress Monroe and I decided to spend my time visiting that and other points till the railroad was completed to Goldsboro.

Many refugees and ex-prisoners had by this time arrived from Sherman's army at Fayetteville. Many of whom went North on the same vessel that I took to Fortress Monroe. Among the passengers was the lieutenant who wrote, "When Sherman Marched Down to the Sea."[4]

I had a good look at Fortress Monroe, then took a boat to Norfolk, and went over to Portsmouth, where I had my first taste of fresh oysters, which were so large that they had to be cut in two before eating. Then I went back to Fort Monroe, where I embarked on a boat for Newbern, N.C.

It has always been a mystery to me how I made that whole trip in Confederate uniform, among strangers, without having been challenged to show my authority for traveling. It is true I had a pass from General Sherman, but was never asked to show it. Neither was I called on to pay passage on any of the boats.

43

Goldsboro

Formerly they boasted of me vainly; with averted eyes
Now they look askance upon me, friends no more but enemies.

ON ARRIVING at Goldsboro, I found the army and the scouts and learned that during my absence they had been having some pretty rough experiences. At Fayetteville, Captain Duncan, who had again been put in charge of the scouts as chief, had been taken prisoner by Wade Hampton's body guard, and White had been again wounded, this time through the left shoulder (the first time at the siege of Atlanta, through the right). This man White proved to be an ungrateful dog, for notwithstanding the fact that he got so much glory in being twice wounded severely, and has now nearly lost his sight, he is robbing the government and capitalists of the magnificent sum of six dollars per month. Such is human nature.

Captain Duncan had succeeded in escaping from Hampton and returned in a most deplorable condition.[1] He had always been rather a dudish and dressy man, but had been stripped of everything and came in without hat or shoes, and only an old shirt and a pair of negro cotton "Osnaburg" breeches. The boys used to say that Hampton took some of his sand as he was afterward more cautious. This was probably a joke because I noticed all of them were a good deal more cautious than formerly, when we had only "Wheeler's thieves" and home guards to contend with.

Wade Hampton was most brutal to all prisoners taken and had announced that he would hang all foragers taken, and I believe did murder seventeen on one occasion, and would have continued that course had not General Kilpatrick retaliated, and Sherman notified him by flag of truce that all such acts would be retaliated by killing two of our prisoners for every one they killed of theirs. This stopped the murdering, but not the cruelty.[2]

There were many of the Confederate generals whom our men respected, but none spoke well of "Brute Hampton."

The scouts had very little to do at Goldsboro, only occasionally making a trip into the country, and then only short distances. Besides, our number was getting small, there being but four remaining for duty, the balance being killed or wounded.

General Sherman paid Amick and me each five hundred dollars for the trip to Wilmington and told us that as soon as places could be found, we should receive promotions, and instructed General Howard to see to this matter.

I think it was on the 6th of April at 10 o'clock P.M. that Amick, Bedoll, and I were called to General Howard's tent, who informed us that his brother, Captain C.H., had been promoted to colonel of a new regiment, and that he would secure for each of us commissions as captain in his regiment, or if we chose, he would promise us a commission as second lieutenant in the Regular Service, but that appointment would, of course, be later. We were told that we must decide by four o'clock next morning, as the colonel would start at that hour for his new regiment and those who chose his service must accompany him.

Amick at once chose the Regular Service, but did not receive his commission till several months later, having to study to pass a rigid examination. That may have been all right from a theoretical standpoint but I want to say that I believe he was then better qualified to handle a company of soldiers in an engagement than he was ten years later after being "transmogrified" into a "regular."

Bedoll chose the Volunteer Service, while I, being undecided, got out my horse and rode several miles to my old regiment, the 32nd Wisconsin, where I called up my captain, Bixby, and took him over to Colonel De Groat's and laid the matter before them. After deliberating over the matter a while, the colonel said, "If you would like to remain in the service the remainder of your life, I would advise you to choose the Regular Service, but if only a short time, I would select the Volunteer Service." That settled the matter for me and I went back and reported at four o'clock to Colonel Howard to accompany him.[3]

We went by rail to Newbern, thence by boat to Baltimore, and thence by rail to New York, where we arrived early in the morning, where as we landed, we heard the newsboys calling. "Morning papers. All about the surrender of General Lee."

While each and every one of the boys looked upon Bedoll as one of the most valuable and trusty scouts, still, inasmuch as he had never done anything to especially attract the attention of the general commanding, it was for a long time a puzzle to us why he was selected for promotion when Collins, White, and Wallace were left out.

In 1885, I called on General Howard in Omaha, and had with him quite an extended conversation, or visit. He asked me the whereabouts of the scouts and I was surprised to learn that he remembered the greater part of them by name. He also asked me if I knew why Bedoll had been promoted and I answered that I supposed that it was because he was a good man, a good scout, and because he was qualified to fill the position assigned him.

He said that while these qualifications were taken into consideration, there was another and, to him more important, reason for his selection, to-wit: that on one occasion while the troops were lying in camp at Goldsboro, one of his staff officers saw a group of soldiers making sport of a poor white woman who had come to the camp to gather up the wasted rations to feed her children. That Bedoll came to her rescue and soundly berated them for their rudeness and then took from his own supply all the provisions he had caused the others to do the same, and gave them to the poor woman, who went away weeping for joy.

On one occasion after the army left Fayetteville, the scouts, after a long, hard day's ride, were compelled to camp in the woods. It was near the entrance to a lane which led to a village a mile or two distant. They had learned that a small force of the enemy were in the village and did not consider themselves strong enough to gather the Johns in. Just at good daylight two of the "rebellious gentlemen" who had apparently been carousing all night were seen coming toward Bedoll, who was on picket at the end of the lane. Joe had no other means of notifying the boys than to call out loudly a challenge, "Halt, yourself, you Yankee something!" They put spurs to their horses and tried to ride over him. Joe waited till they got to the proper distance, then fired and one of them fell off his horse dead. The other one pulled up his horse and retreated hastily. Joe could have killed him also, and when asked why he didn't, said, "We don't want to kill the whole Confederacy."

Bedoll differed from all the other scouts in that he never got rattled, never made any bad breaks, and never permitted pleasure to interfere with business. He was as homely as Lincoln, and had he been older, I think would have closely resembled him. Poor Joe, I have learned that that dread disease, consumption, accomplished what the Confederacy failed to do.

Conclusion

No more is heard the trumpet's brazen road,
Sweet sleep is banished from our eyes no more.

DURING THE MARCH to the Sea, all buildings of a public nature, such as cotton-gins, corn mills, factories of every sort, fences and bridges, as well as railroads and telegraphs, were destroyed by order of division and corps commanders. There were probably a few private houses also burned by foragers through wantonness. This last was strictly against orders and would have been severely punished if the perpetrators had been caught in the act.

On the Carolina Campaign, things were entirely different. While all buildings of public utility were destroyed, nearly half of the private buildings were also set on fire, not by order of anyone in authority, but by soldiers and refugee negroes. While this also was against orders, there seemed to be no effort being made to stop it.

It was reported throughout the army that General Logan had issued a special order to the 15th Corps, *"Positively prohibiting under penalty of death, the setting on fire any fence or building when an ordnance train was passing."*

I presume that this was a false report, but at any rate it caused a general laugh whenever repeated.

By gaining an elevated piece of land, we could always look off to the left for many miles and tell exactly how far away and how far advanced were the different columns by the lines of smoke ascending along their lines of march.

There were, no doubt, hundreds and perhaps thousands, of innocent families who suffered by these unnecessary and wanton acts. It was extremely probable that only a small minority of the people of that unfortunate state were really responsible for the deluging of the land with a bloody war. I have since become quite well acquainted with many people of South Carolina and found them to be as good people, good neighbors, and good citizens as those of any other state. South Carolina was to the South what Massachusetts was to the North, that is, they did the talking and wanted others to do the acting.

It was a common remark by the soldiers of all armies, North and South, and especially those of the West, that the two states ought to be compelled to fight it out.

I recall an incident, when, two days out from Columbia, Amick and I came to a neat house by the roadside with no negro quarters in sight. A lady was on the porch wringing her hands and seeming to be in great distress. By her side was a beautiful little girl of about four years of age. This was between two of the main columns. She could see the smoke to the right and left but as yet had seen no Federal soldiers.

Terrible stories were told in advance of the army, of its depredations, and with few exceptions women were frightened nearly out of their wits. We rode up to the gate and inquired the cause of her alarm and she told us amidst her sobs of her fears. We assured her they were groundless—that the worst that could happen would be the taking of her provisions and chickens.

She informed us that her husband was not in the army, but was a Baptist preacher, and that this was the parsonage of that denomination. Her husband was, she stated, then hiding in the swamps till our army passed. We told her to call him up and we would see that he was not troubled, but she did not succeed in locating him. Her fright had been so great that when we left, she was trembling like one with a palsy.

At another time—I think it was the day we crossed the Catawba River—we halted at a small planter's house and asked to get some dinner. There was no one at home but the madam and her grown daughter. They had no slaves and were fairly well educated and intelligent. We told them that we were Yankees, but they could scarcely believe us. The young lady said she had been to Florence a few weeks previously and seen very many Yankees, but that they did not look like us. They expressed as much horror at the barbarity with which our soldiers, when prisoners, were treated as any Northern lady could have done. In about an hour they had prepared for us as good a dinner as anyone could wish. They appeared to be very sociable, having not a particle of the bitterness sometimes heard and seen in the

South, and when we left, we could not but wish and hope that this family would be exempt from the misfortune met by many.

Judge of our grief when after riding a mile and ascending a hill, on looking back we saw that identical house in flames.

I do not possess the ability or language to discuss this feature of the war. This unnecessary destruction of property that could do the Confederacy no good and us no harm was deplored by a very large majority of our army. It was the scalawags that are always present in armies that brought disgrace to better men. I want to also say here that it was not the private soldiers alone who were guilty of these dastardly acts. Some line officers have also been known to be equally guilty.

In support of my theory that a certain percentage of all armies are bad men at heart, I submit the following from Confederate authority, to show that the scalawags of our army were not more numerous than in theirs.

Extracts from a letter to the Confederate Secretary of War, published in the Charleston *Courier* of January 10, 1865, and in the Charleston *Mercury* (tri-weekly) of January 11th:

> I cannot forbear appealing to you on behalf of the producing population of the States of Georgia and South Carolina for protection against the destructive lawlessness of members of General Wheeler's Command. From Augusta to Hardeville, the road is now strewn with corn left on the ground unconsumed. Beeves have been shot down in the field, one quarter taken off and the balance left for the buzzards. Horses are stolen out of wagons on the road, and by wholesale out of the stables at night. Within a few miles of this neighborhood, Wheeler's men tried to rob a young lady of a horse while she was on a visit to a neighbor's, but for the timely arrival of a citizen, who prevented the outrage being perpetrated. It is no unusual sight to see these men ride late into camp with all sorts of plunder. Private houses are visited; carpets, blankets and other furniture they can lay their hands on are taken by force in the presence of the owners, etc.

The following is from the Savannah *Republican*, of October 1864:

> It is notorious that our own army while falling back from Dalton was even more dreaded by the inhabitants than the army of Sherman.

The soldiers and even the officers, took everything that came in their way, giving the excuse that if they did not, the enemy would. Subsequently stragglers from our own army almost sacked the stores in Atlanta. Now complaints loud and deep come up from that portion of Georgia in the neighborhood of our Army, telling of outrages committed by straggling squads of Cavalry, and of insults offered to the families of the best and most patriotic citizens.

The Richmond *Enquirer* of October 6, 1864, contained the following with reference to Early's command in the Valley of Virginia. After speaking of the drunkenness habitual among them, from the chief downward, its correspondent says:

> The cavalry forces that had been operating in the Valley, and flittin hither and thither along the Potomac and Shenandoah, were already demoralized, and since their last visit to Maryland they have been utterly worthless. They were in the habit of robbing friend and foe alike. They have been known to strip Virginia women of all they had—widows whose sons were in our army—and then to burn their houses. At Hancock, in western Maryland, they stopped a minister of the Gospel in the street on the Sabbath day, and made him stand and deliver his money. These monstrous truths are stated in the official report of the officer commanding a part of these cavalry forces.

The following is from the Richmond *Whig*, being part of a letter of a correspondent of that paper soon after Sherman marched north from Columbia. Republished in *Army and Navy Journal*, March 18, 1865. Speaking of the Confederate evacuation of Columbia, S.C., the writer says:

> The worst feature of the whole scene occurred on the day of which I write. A party of Wheeler's cavalry, accompanied by their officers, dashed into town, tied their horses, and as systematically as if they had been bred to the business, proceeded to break into the stores along Main Street and rob them of their contents. Under these circumstances you may well imagine that our people would rather see the Yankees, or old Satan himself, than a party of the aforesaid Wheeler's Cavalry. The barbarities committed by some of them are represented to be frightful.

I remember that during our march in North Carolina, we frequently found issues of a North Carolina *Weekly* newspaper, which published many humorous sketches on incidents of the war. I recall one story that caused much amusement at headquarters. It described a scene at Fredericksburg after one of our repulses at that place.

There had been a long cold spell when the soldiers on each side were busy keeping warm, so there had been no "joshing" each other across the picket line as had been the custom. At length better weather prevailed and the pickets renewed their chaffing, and the following dialogue took place across the river.

> REB. Halloa, Yank.
> YANK. Halloa.
> REB. What's the news over there?
> YANK. We've got a new general.
> REB. Who is it?
> YANK. General Sickles.
> (*After an interval of silence it was again resumed.*)
> YANK. Halloa, John.
> REB. Halloa.
> YANK. I say, John, we are coming over there in a few days and
>   lick hell out of you.
> REB. Halloa, Yank.
> YANK. Halloa.
> REB. Say, Yank, tell General Sickles to bring his wife along.

The reader will notice that I have made use of the word "rebel" as little as possible, and then only to avoid repetition. I have never liked the word because of its misuse. I have noticed that all men since the beginning of history, who have objected to the tyranny of their rulers, have been called "rebels."

All unsuccessful revolutions have been called rebellious, while the participants of the successful ones have been spoken of as patriots. It makes a great deal of difference as to "whose ox is gored." Besides the highest authority in our land, the courts, as well as some of our most able lawyers and statesmen, have declared that, while our Constitution did not specially recognize the right of secession, it did not specially forbid it, leaving it an open question.

When the attorney general decided that Jeff Davis could not be convicted, under our constitution, of the charge of treason, that settled it so far as the word "rebel" is concerned.

Then, again, I have disliked the word, because it was a common epithet, hurled by every Englishman at every American for a hundred years, and became as it were, to us, a word of honor instead of one of contempt.

Since its coinage, it had always been to kings and the nobility, what the word "heretic" has been to the church. It has always been an anathema used by the oppressor to the oppressed.

NOTES

Introduction

1. Society of the Army of the Tennessee, "Report of the Proceedings of the Annual Meeting of the Society of the Army of the Tennessee," 1869, 359.

2. A memoir by one of Quimby's fellow scouts is James Pike, *The Scout and Ranger: Being the Personal Adventures of Corporal Pike, of the Fourth Ohio Cavalry. As a Texan Ranger, in the Indian Wars, Delineating Western Adventure; Afterwards a Scout and Spy, in Tennessee, Alabama, Georgia, and the Carolinas, under General Mitchell, Rosecrans, Stanley, Sheridan, Lytle, Thomas, Crook, and Sherman. Fully Illustrating the Secret Service. Twenty-Five Full-Page Engravings* (Cincinnati and New York, J. R. Hawley & Co., 1865).

3. Robert P. Broadwater, *Civil War Special Forces: The Elite and Distinct Fighting Units of the Union and Confederate Armies* (Santa Barbara: Praeger, 2014); William Gilmore Beymer, *Scouts and Spies of the Civil War* (Lincoln: University of Nebraska Press, 2003). Introduction by William B. Feis, xv–xxiii.

4. Edwin C Fishel, *The Secret War for the Union: The Untold Story of Military Intelligence in the Civil War* (Boston: Houghton Mifflin, 1996), 3–7.

5. Gordon L Olson, *The Notorious Isaac Earl and His Scouts: Union Soldiers, Prisoners, Spies* (Grand Rapids: William B. Eerdmans Publishing Company, 2014), 8–12. Darl L Stephenson, *Headquarters in the Brush: Blazer's Independent Union Scouts* (Athens: Ohio University Press, 2001).

6. Quimby was not alone in blaming excessive theft and violence on "bad apples." Rubin, *Through the Heart of Dixie*, 112–14.

7. William T. Sherman, Special Field Orders No. 15, November 9, 1864. http://cwnc. omeka.chass.ncsu.edu/items/show/145.

8. Two works that carefully explore the nature of these interactions are Jacqueline Glass Campbell, *When Sherman Marched North from the Sea* (Chapel Hill: University of North Carolina Press, 2003), and Lisa Tendrich Frank, *The Civilian War: Confederate Women and Union Soldiers During Sherman's March* (Baton Rouge: Louisiana State University Press, 2015).

9. Joseph T. Glatthaar, *The March to the Sea and Beyond* (Baton Rouge: Louisiana State University Press, 1985), 52–65; Rubin, *Through the Heart of Dixie*, 69–93. The *Visualizing Emancipation* website graphically shows the relationship between the March and emancipation. http://dsl.richmond.edu/emancipation/.

10. On the social and political significance of the GAR, see Stuart McConnell, *Glorious Contentment: The Grand Army of the Republic, 1865–1900* (Chapel Hill: University of North Carolina Press, 1992). On the role of veterans shaping memories of the Civil War, see David W. Blight, *Race and Reunion: The Civil War in American Memory* (Cambridge, Mass.: Belknap Press of Harvard University Press, 2001); Caroline E. Janney,

Remembering the Civil War: Reunion and the Limits of Reconciliation (Chapel Hill: University of North Carolina Press, 2013).

11. Recently, historians have argued that Civil War veterans struggled in their postwar lives, affected to varying degrees by forces akin to post-traumatic stress. For some examples of this literature, see Eric T. Dean, *Shook over Hell: Post-Traumatic Stress, Vietnam, and the Civil War* (Cambridge, Mass.: Harvard University Press, 1997); James Alan Marten, *Sing Not War: The Lives of Union and Confederate Veterans in Gilded Age America* (Chapel Hill: University of North Carolina Press, 2011); Brian Matthew Jordan, *Marching Home: Union Veterans and Their Unending Civil War* (New York: W. W. Norton & Company, 2014).

12. http://www.quimbycentral.com/SonsofBenjamin7Q.html; Omar Alonso Quimby, FindAGrave.com http://www.findagrave.com/cgi-bin/fg.cgi?page=gr&GRid=17525082; Quimby Family Tree.

13. "Reminiscences of Old Time," *Marion (WI) Advertiser*, May 11, 1917. http://www.wigenweb.org/waupaca/News/waupnews1917.htm.

14. NPS Soldiers and Sailors Database; 1860 Manuscript Census; "Reminiscences of Old Time."

15. Compiled service record.

16. Alanson Wood, *History of the 32nd Regiment, Wisconsin Infantry*, n.d.; Records from Dyer, *Compendium*, http://www.civilwararchive.com/Unreghst/unwiinf3.htm#32-ndinf; E[dwin] B[entley] Quiner, *The Military History of Wisconsin* . . . (Chicago: Clarke & Co., 1866); John Norton and Nancy Jane Calenberg, *The Norton Civil War Letters* (Baltimore: PublishAmerica, 2004).

17. Wood, *History of the 32nd Regiment*; Quiner, *Military History of Wisconsin*, 802; Norton and Calenberg.

18. Quimby, "A Prisoner of War," 4–5.

19. Ibid., 6.

20. Ibid., 9–10.

21. Ibid., 11–12.

22. Ibid., 13–18; Compiled Service Records.

23. Wood, *History of the 32nd Regiment*.

24. Wood, *History of the 32nd Regiment*; Quiner, *Military History of Wisconsin*, 803–4.

25. Quiner, *Military History of Wisconsin*, 805.

26. Two recent works dealing extensively with the Union's occupation of Atlanta are Stephen Davis, *What the Yankees Did to Us: Sherman's Bombardment and Wrecking of Atlanta* (Macon, Ga.: Mercer University Press, 2012); Wendy Hammond Venet, *A Changing Wind: Commerce & Conflict in Civil War Atlanta* (New Haven: Yale University Press, 2014). William T. Sherman to James M. Calhoun et al., September 12, 1865 in Brooks D. Simpson and Jean V. Berlin, eds., *Sherman's Civil War: Selected Correspondence of William T. Sherman, 1860–1865* (Chapel Hill: University of North Carolina Press, 1999), 707–9.

27. There are dozens of detailed histories of Sherman's March; here are a few

well-suited to general readers. On the entire march, see Burke Davis, *Sherman's March* (New York: Random House, 1980); Glatthaar, *The March to the Sea and Beyond*. On Georgia specifically, see Anne J. Bailey, *War and Ruin: William T. Sherman and the Savannah Campaign* (Wilmington: Scholarly Resources, 2003); Noah Andre Trudeau, *Southern Storm: Sherman's March to the Sea* (New York: Harper, 2008). For the Carolinas campaign, see John Gilchrist Barrett, *Sherman's March through the Carolinas* (Chapel Hill: University of North Carolina Press, 1956); John M. Gibson, *Those 163 Days; a Southern Account of Sherman's March from Atlanta to Raleigh* (New York: Coward-McCann, 1961). Sherman's own *Memoirs* also offer a uniquely readable overview, *Memoirs of General William T. Sherman* (Bloomington: Indiana University Press, 1957).

28. *The War of the Rebellion: A Compilation of the Official Records of the Union and Confederate Armies* [hereafter OR] Series I, Vol. 39, Part 3, 713–14; Sherman, *Memoirs*, 175–76.

29. On the interactions between Sherman's men and civilians, see Frank, *The Civilian War*; Campbell, *When Sherman Marched North from the Sea*; and Rubin, *Through the Heart of Dixie*.

30. Wills, *Army Life of an Illinois Soldier*, 324.

31. James C. Bonner, *Milledgeville: Georgia's Antebelleum Capital* (Athens: University of Georgia Press, 1978); Hugh T. Harrington, *Civil War Milledgeville: Tales from the Confederate Capital of Georgia* (Charleston: History Press, 2005).

32. John K Derden, *The World's Largest Prison: The Story of Camp Lawton* (Macon, Ga.: Mercer University Press, 2012).

33. Roger S. Durham, *Guardian of Savannah: Fort McAllister, Georgia, in the Civil War and Beyond*, *Studies in Maritime History* (Columbia, SC: University of South Carolina Press, 2008).

34. Telegram from General William T. Sherman to President Abraham Lincoln announcing the surrender of Savannah, Georgia, as a Christmas present to the President. The National Archives, https://research.archives.gov/id/301637.

35. Wood, *History of the 32nd Regiment*; Quiner, *Military History of Wisconsin*, 805.

36. Sherman, *Memoirs*, 254.

37. Wood, *History of the 32nd Regiment*.

38. The question of who burned Columbia, Union soldiers or retreating Confederates, has been controversial for the last 150 years. For the Confederate viewpoint, see William Gilmore Simms and David Aiken, *A City Laid Waste: The Capture, Sack, and Destruction of the City of Columbia* (Columbia: University of South Carolina Press, 2005). A more balanced perspective can be found in Marion Brunson Lucas, *Sherman and the Burning of Columbia* (College Station: Texas A & M University Press, 1976).

39. Bentonville has been the subject of several monographs, including Broadwater, *Battle of Despair*; Hughes, *Bentonville: The Final Battle of Sherman and Johnston*; and Mark L. Bradley, *Last Stand in the Carolinas*.

40. Mark L. Bradley, *This Astounding Close: The Road to the Bennett Place* (Chapel Hill: University of North Carolina Press, 2000).

41. Anne Sarah Rubin, "The Grand Review of Sherman's Bummers," *The Conversation*, May 25, 2015. https://theconversation.com/the-grand-review-of-shermans-bummers-41555.

42. Wood, *History of the 32nd Regiment*.

43. Compiled Service Record; 1882 Army Record.

44. Pension records; Lottie Roeder Roth, *History of Whatcom County*, Vol. II (Chicago: Pioneer Historical Pub. Co., 1926), 378–79.

45. Roth, *History of Whatcom County*, 379; "Verdigre, Nebraska," *Virtual Nebraska*, http://www.casde.unl.edu/history/counties/knox/verdigre/.

46. George W. Quimby, "Captured by Forrest," *National Tribune*, July 2, 1903.

47. Pension records.

Chapter 1

1. While the literature on spies in the Civil War is voluminous, much less has been written about the role of scouts specifically. The most recent treatment of scouts can be found in Robert P. Broadwater, *Civil War Special Forces: The Elite and Distinct Fighting Units of the Union and Confederate Armies*, 2014.

2. On the siege and occupation of Atlanta, see Wendy Hammond Venet, *A Changing Wind: Commerce & Conflict in Civil War Atlanta* (New Haven: Yale University Press, 2014); Stephen Davis, *What the Yankees Did to Us: Sherman's Bombardment and Wrecking of Atlanta* (Macon, Ga.: Mercer University Press, 2012).

3. On September 7, Sherman informed Confederate General John Bell Hood of his plan to expel all civilians from Atlanta, so that he would not need to guard his men from possible attacks, he would not need to feed the civilians, and finally he would not be required to leave troops behind to hold the city. In this letter, he also offered a brief truce to enable Hood's soldiers to help move the Confederate families. Hood's response to this is well known—he proclaimed the plan to be "unprecedented . . . in studied and ingenious cruelty." Sherman and Hood traded barbs through a series of letters, debating whether the expulsion violated the laws of war or not. While they disagreed on that point, Hood did agree to the armistice. When it ended after ten days, Hood moved his 39,000-man Army of the Tennessee from the area around Lovejoy's Station to Palmetto. Finally, on September 29, the Confederate crossed the Chattahoochee and moved into North Georgia, to strike at the Union's supply lines along the Western and Atlantic Railroad. Sherman and Hood's correspondence can be found in United States et al., *The War of the Rebellion: A Compilation of the Official Records of the Union and Confederate Armies* (Washington, DC: Government Printing Office, 1880), Vol. 39, Part 2, 4414–22; Davis, *What the Yankees Did to Us*, 297, 345.

4. I believe this is a reference to Lewis F. Dayton, who served first as one of Sherman's aides de camp and then later as his adjutant general. See William T. Sherman, *Memoirs of General William T. Sherman* (Bloomington: Indiana University Press, 1957), 178.

5. On guerrillas in the Civil War in general, see Daniel E Sutherland, *A Savage Conflict: The Decisive Role of Guerrillas in the American Civil War* (Chapel Hill: University of North Carolina Press, 2013).

6. As Quimby explains, Sherman divided his army into two wings, each one comprised of two corps. General Oliver O. Howard commanded the Right Wing, with General Peter J. Osterhaus at the head of the XV Corps and General Francis Preston Blair Jr. in charge of the XVII Corps. General Henry W. Slocum headed the Left Wing, with General Jefferson C. Davis (no relation to the Confederate president) in charge of the XIV Corps, and General Alpheus S. Williams at the head of the XX Corps. The cavalry was led by General Judson Kilpatrick.

7. The National Park Service Civil War Soldiers and Sailors Database http://www.nps.gov/civilwar/soldiers-and-sailors-database.htm lists a Patterson Wallace in the 58th Indiana Infantry, which marched with Sherman. That regiment had a Michael Daugherty on its rolls, but not an Ed. Possible Edward Daughertys could be found in the 17th Wisconsin, 32nd Ohio, 11th Iowa, and 31st Iowa.

8. Can't find a match.

9. This actually appears to be Joseph A. Bedoll of the 47th Ohio. Like Quimby, Bedoll later served as an officer for the 128th U.S.C.T. http://www.nps.gov/civilwar/soldiers-and-sailors-database.htm.

10. Names are too common to find.

11. Burns is probably Barney Burns of the 8th Indiana Cavalry; can't find the right Dawson.

12. "Contraband" refers to a former slave who ran away to Union lines. These people were considered free under the laws regarding contraband of war. At least 25,000 of these so-called contrabands followed Sherman's army at one time during the March.

13. According to Sherman's Special Field Orders No. 120, each brigade was supposed to send out parties of foragers, whose explicit job was to gather food for the soldiers each day. In theory, this was a check or control: foodstuffs were to be seized in an orderly and systemic fashion. While these regularized parties were sent out, they were often followed by less organized bands of "bummers," operating with few controls. Special Field Orders No. 120 in *OR*, Vol. 39, Part 3, 713–14.

14. This is most likely a reference to the Right Wing crossing the river at Ball's Ferry on November 26, after several days of skirmishing. Trudeau, *Southern Storm*, 232, 251–55, 264.

15. General Joseph Wheeler commanded the cavalry branch of the Confederate Army of the Tennessee. His 8,000 man force provided the main opposition to Sherman's March, along with some units of Georgia Militia. Because Quimby and his companions were often out in advance of the main march, they frequently ran into Wheeler's men.

16. Quimby is probably referring to a few notorious incidents during the March, where prisoners were killed. He refers specifically to one in Chapter 43.

Chapter 2

1. Most likely Quimby meant Lieutenant Amos J. Griffin, of the 5th Kentucky Cavalry, as indicated in United States et al., *The War of the Rebellion: A Compilation of the Official Records of the Union and Confederate Armies* (Washington, DC: Government Printing Office, 1880), Vol. 44, Part 1, 379.

2. Jonesboro is about twenty miles south of Atlanta, in Clayton County.

3. On November 15, as his troops began to move out of the city on the March, Sherman ordered that everything of military value be burned. About one third of the city wound up destroyed, primarily the business district. Anne Sarah Rubin, *Through the Heart of Dixie: Sherman's March and American Memory*, 2014, 10.

Chapter 3

1. This refers to the Battle of Atlanta, which was followed by the six-week siege of the city.

Chapter 4

1. He would have been one of the refugees who left Atlanta under Sherman's orders, prompting the exchange of letters between Sherman and Hood. See Stephen Davis, *What the Yankees Did to Us: Sherman's Bombardment and Wrecking of Atlanta* (Macon, Ga.: Mercer University Press, 2012), 290–330; Wendy Venet, *A Changing Wind: Commerce and Conflict in Civil War Atlanta* (New Haven: Yale University Press, 2014), 174–78.

2. In other words, that he had been captured and sent to the notorious Confederate prison, under the command of Henry Wirz.

3. Milledgeville, the capital of Georgia until 1868.

Chapter 5

1. On November 18, the Georgia State Legislature hastily adjourned and fled the capital. The Governor, Joe Brown, brought in prisoners from the state penitentiary to pack up the executive mansion and departed the following day. Trudeau, *Southern Storm*, 130, 150–51.

2. Presumably Robert Collins of the 15th Illinois Cavalry.

3. General Howard to General Sherman, November 21, 1864, *OR*, Series 1, Vol. 44, 509.

4. In other words, be returned to regular infantry service.

Chapter 6

1. In the flurry of activity leading up to Sherman's arrival in Milledgeville, several hundred prisoners were offered their freedom in exchange for a promise to fight off the invaders. They were under the control of Georgia's state adjutant and inspector general,

Henry C. Wayne. The prisoners who remained set the penitentiary on fire once Union troops had taken the town. Bailey, *War and Ruin*, 67–68.

2. Possibly Henry W. Conklin of the 4th Michigan Cavalry.

Chapter 7

1. Surprisingly, Quimby makes no mention of Griswoldville, the only real battle of the Georgia Campaign. Soldiers from the Right Wing fought Georgia militiamen near Gordon. When the smoke of battle cleared, the Union troops were dismayed to realize they had been fighting boys and old men. No one else remained to try to stop them. William Harris Bragg, *Griswoldville* (Macon, Ga.: Mercer University Press, 2000).

2. In the original manuscript, Quimby refers to an accompanying map, which was not found.

Chapter 10

1. Sherman's troops often killed dogs on plantations. See Rubin, *Through the Heart of Dixie*, 51.

2. In the anecdote that Grant relates, a Southern matron chastises a soldier for taking her poodle away, explaining it was not a bloodhound. "'Well, madam, we cannot tell what it will grow into if we leave it behind,' said the soldier as he went off with it." Ulysses S. Grant, *Personal Memoirs of Ulysses S. Grant (1885)*, Vol. 11, 364–65.

Chapter 11

1. Captain Duncan's report, via General Howard's adjutant, can be found in *Official Records*, Series 1, Vol. 44, 578.

2. In a note to Howard's adjutant, General Blair tartly commented that "Captain Duncan, commanding scouts from your headquarters, and the two of his men who were shot were disgustingly drunk to-day, and that had they been sober his men probably would not have been wounded." *OR*, Series 1, Vol. 44, 622.

Chapter 12

1. The prisoners to which Quimby refers were Union soldiers who had been moved to the hastily constructed Camp Lawton built on the outskirts of Millen. Camp Lawton was only in operation for six weeks during the early fall of 1864, but had the dubious distinction of briefly being the Confederacy's largest prison camp. It was built to house overflow from Andersonville. By the time its prisoners were evacuated days before the March came through, over 700 men had died. Many of the prisoners who were moved wound up in the prison camp at Florence, South Carolina. Sherman's men were so angry at seeing the conditions in Camp Lawton that they burned much of Millen in retaliation. See John K Derden, *The World's Largest Prison: The Story of Camp Lawton* (Macon, Ga.: Mercer University Press, 2012).

Chapter 13

1. Historically, the Wiregrass region of Georgia stretched from the Chattahoochee river to Savannah, and was known for its sandy soil, pine forests, and wiregrass. The land was ill-suited to cotton production, and therefore in the 1860s was sparsely populated, with small farms as opposed to large plantations. Mark Wetherington, "Wiregrass Georgia," *The New Georgia Encyclopedia*, http://www.georgiaencyclopedia.org/articles/geography-environment/wiregrass-georgia.

Chapter 15

1. It's impossible to quantify the number of sexual assaults along the route of Sherman's March. The number reported is surely much lower than the actual number; African American women were certainly subject to more assaults than white women. Significantly, white women's fear of sexual assault was quite high, and shaped their overall responses to and memories of the March. See 1, 109–12; Rubin, *Through the Heart of Dixie*, 48–50.

2. This, along with his trip through the lines to Wilmington, North Carolina, is the best known and best documented of Quimby's exploits. For a narrative account, see Noah Andre Trudeau, *Southern Storm: Sherman's March to the Sea* (New York: Harper, 2008), 390–91, 401–2, 410–12. Trudeau drew his version from Charles H. Howard's *Incidents and Operations Connected with the Capture of Savannah* (Chicago: Cozzens & Beaton Company, 1891), and a 1925 *National Tribune* article. The Ossabaw Sound mission also appears in both General Sherman's and General Howard's official reports, *OR*, Series 1, Vol. 44, 11, 72. Howard's contemporaneous note of the mission can be found in *OR*, Series 1, Vol. 44, 11, 671.

Chapter 16

1. An important crossing point on the Ogeechee River. On December 13, the XV Corps crossed here, on their way to taking Fort McAllister. Trudeau, *Southern Storm*, 422.

2. Fort McAllister's earthenworks guarded the mouth of the Ogeechee River, fifteen miles south of Savannah. It was constructed in 1861 and had been designed to absorb attacks from the water. Thus, Sherman rightly concluded that it was vulnerable to attack from land. For a detailed look at Fort McAllister during and after the war, see Roger S. Durham, *Guardian of Savannah: Fort McAllister, Georgia, in the Civil War and Beyond*, *Studies in Maritime History* (Columbia, SC: University of South Carolina Press, 2008). On p. 129, Durham misidentifies Quimby as George W. Quinn of the 31st Illinois.

3. Durham, *Guardian of Savannah*, 23–24, 48, 129–31.

Chapter 17

1. Quimby is probably referring to tabby, a building material used in this area made of a mixture of lime, ash, sand, water, and oyster shells.

2. The first ship Quimby et al. encountered was the *USS Flag.* Then they were quickly moved to the *USS Dandelion.* On the naval blockade and the ships around Savannah, see Robert M. Browning, *Success Is All That Was Expected: The South Atlantic Blockading Squadron during the Civil War* (Washington, DC: Brassey's, Inc., 2002), 334–35.

3. This indicates that Quimby wrote these memoirs around 1901.

Chapter 18

1. Quimby appears to be in error here—the 12th was a Monday.

2. Another error of memory by Quimby: In his memoirs, Sherman refers to Dahlgren's flagship as the *Harvest Moon.* William T. Sherman, *Memoirs of General William T. Sherman* (Bloomington: Indiana University Press, 1957), 200.

Chapter 20

1. Sherman, *Memoirs*, 200–1.

2. This was the rice plantation belonging to Dr. Langdon Cheves, on the north bank of the Ogeechee. Durham, *Guardian of Savannah*, 130; Noah Andre Trudeau, *Southern Storm: Sherman's March to the Sea* (New York: Harper, 2008), 408.

Chapter 21

1. Slang for supply line.

Chapter 22

1. Confederate forces under the command of General William Hardee withdrew from Savannah and moved across the Savannah River into South Carolina.

Chapter 23

1. Sherman was beginning to move his armies into place for the Carolinas Campaign. Just as he had misled Confederates into thinking that his Georgia targets might have included Macon and Augusta, so, too, he hoped to feint toward Augusta and Charleston, while heading for Columbia the whole time.

2. This battle was fought on November 30, 1864. For a brief description, see Trudeau, *Southern Storm*, 290–300.

3. Colonel James T. Conklin, not to be confused with the Conklin mentioned earlier in Quimby's narrative.

Chapter 24

1. General Sherman himself understood that the tenor of the campaign would change in South Carolina. As he recalled in his *Memoirs*, "Somehow our men had got the idea that South Carolina was the cause of all our troubles; her people were the first to fire on Fort Sumter, had been in a great hurry to precipitate the country into civil

war; and therefore on them should fall the scourge of war in its worst form. . . . I saw and felt that we would not be able longer to restrain our men as we had done in Georgia . . . and I would not restrain the army lest its vigor and energy should be impaired." William T. Sherman, *Memoirs of General William T. Sherman* (Bloomington: Indiana University Press, 1957), 254.

2. Sherman had two main objectives for the Carolinas Campaign: First, to continue to strike at the heart and morale of the Confederacy by destroying railroads, supplies, and other infrastructure; and second, to move his army into Virginia, where their ultimate goal was to reinforce Grant's Army, still stuck in the Petersburg trenches.

3. As on the Georgia Campaign, Sherman divided his army into two wings, with the Right commanded by General Howard and the Left by General Slocum. The XV and the XVII Corps, commanded by Generals Logan and Blair, respectively, comprised the Right Wing; the XIV and the XX under Generals Davis and Williams made up the Left. General Kilpatrick continued to command the cavalry. The Right Wing had massed at Pocotaligo, South Carolina, about forty-five miles north of Savannah; the Left was organized at Sister's Ferry, a crossing about forty miles upstream on the Savannah River.

4. Quimby's account of his and John White's capture by, and escape from, Confederate General Nathan Bedford Forrest's forces was published in the *National Tribune* (Washington, DC) on June 25, 1903.

5. Sherman's pioneer corps was made up of newly emancipated African American men. While Sherman was unwilling to feed or otherwise support freed women and children, he was happy to use able-bodied men for clearing and building roads.

Chapter 25

1. In June 1865, Quimby was discharged from the 32nd Wisconsin, and commissioned as a second lieutenant in the 128th United States Colored Troops, a regiment comprised of newly freed African Americans. He served with them in South Carolina through July 1866.

2. The Battle of Rivers Bridge, fought on February 2–3, 1865, was the most significant engagement of the march through South Carolina. About 1,400 Confederates under Confederate General Lafayette McLaws tried to hold off members of the Right Wing. On February 3, two brigades waded through the swamp and flanked McLaws's men, forcing them to withdraw to Branchville. In the end, although the battle has been hailed as one of the "last stands" against Sherman and his men, it only delayed them for one day. Christopher G. Crabb, *Facing Sherman in South Carolina: March through the Swamps* (Charleston, SC: History Press, 2010), 48–59.

3. If Quimby is referring specifically to the number of casualties his regiments took at Rivers Bridge, he is mistaken. All together, the Union had 92 casualties, the Confederates 170. http://www.nps.gov/hps/abpp/battles/sc011.htm.

Chapter 26

1. Sergeant Benjamin F. Sheldon, 32nd Wisconsin. Listed in *Wisconsin Losses in the Civil War*.

2. Wager Swayne, Colonel of the 43rd Ohio, made a brevet brigadier general on ·February 5, 1865, and was given full rank a month later. Grenville Mellen Dodge and Military Order of the Loyal Legion of the United States. New York Commmandery, *Sketch of the Military Service of Major General Wager Swayne* (New York, 1903).

3. Union veterans often recalled treating Confederate children with kindness, and Southern stories of Sherman's March also often made reference to these kinds of interaction. Rubin, *Through the Heart of Dixie*, 65–66, 117–18.

4. Quimby's condemnation of foragers is rather surprising, given his own descriptions of drinking and taking food. It's also unusual, given the way that Sherman's bummers were generally celebrated after the war, often portrayed as good-natured scamps with a wink and a nod. See Rubin, *Through the Heart of Dixie*, 94–120.

5. This paternalistic thread was woven through white reactions to emancipation. For examples, see Leon F. Litwack, *Been in the Storm So Long: The Aftermath of Slavery* (New York: Knopf: distributed by Random House, 1979); Thavolia Glymph, *Out of the House of Bondage: The Transformation of the Plantation Household* (Cambridge and New York: Cambridge University Press, 2008).

Chapter 27

1. On the contentious relationships between Sherman's soldiers and Southern white women, see Jacqueline Glass Campbell, *When Sherman Marched North from the Sea* (Chapel Hill: University of North Carolina Press, 2003); Lisa Tendrich Frank, *The Civilian War: Confederate Women and Union Soldiers During Sherman's March* (Baton Rouge: Louisiana State University Press, 2015).

2. Quimby is reflecting what became a powerful trope in post–Civil War literature: the marriage between a Union soldier and a Southern white woman. Historian Nina Silber has argued that these romances represented the masculine North taming the defeated and feminized South. Nina Silber, *The Romance of Reunion: Northerners and the South, 1865–1900* (Chapel Hill: University of North Carolina Press, 1993).

Chapter 28

1. Quimby's portrayal of the March as generally pleasant comports well with the recollections of his fellow veterans. Rubin, *Through the Heart of Dixie*, 94–120.

Chapter 29

1. Sherman never had any intention of trying to capture Charleston. In a letter to General Grant, dated December 24,1864, Sherman laid out his reasoning, explaining that "Charleston is now a mere desolated wreck, and is hardly worth the time it would

take to starve it out." Furthermore, Sherman's plan was to head for Raleigh, ideally forcing Lee out of Petersburg to come to the North Carolina capital's defense. Sherman, *Memoirs*, 225. Davis, *Sherman's March*, 142.

Chapter 30

1. Sherman's General Order No. 26, written on February 16, 1865, ordered General Howard's XV Corps to cross the Saluda and Broad Rivers and enter the city of Columbia, occupy the city, and "destroy the public buildings, railroad property, manufacturing and machine shops," while "[sparing] libraries, asylums, and private dwellings." This was not what happened, as fire broke out and about one third of the city was destroyed. Southern poet William Gilmore Simms published an account of his experiences in Columbia during the burning; a classic account by a historian is Marion Brunson Lucas, *Sherman and the Burning of Columbia* (College Station: Texas A & M University Press, 1976). William Gilmore Simms and David Aiken, *A City Laid Waste: The Capture, Sack, and Destruction of the City of Columbia* (Columbia: University of South Carolina Press, 2005).

2. Captain Francis De Gress of the 1st Illinois Light Artillery, Battery H, which became known as De Gress' Battery. See *OR*, 47, Vol. 1, 20–21, 197, 227, 271.

3. Quimby could easily be referring to the account published by Sherman's aide Major George W. Nichols. In *The Story of the Great March*, Nichols compares the Saluda mill workers unfavorably to the famous Lowell mill girls, condemning them as "unkempt, frowzy, ragged, dirty, and all together ignorant and wretched." George Ward Nichols, *The Story of the Great March* (New York: Harper & Brothers, 1865), 158; Marion Brunson Lucas, *Sherman and the Burning of Columbia* (College Station: Texas A & M University Press, 1976), 73–73.

Chapter 31

1. The controversy over the burning of Columbia has been well researched and argued. Ultimately, most historians have decided that both the Confederate and the Union bore some responsibility. James Ford Rhodes, "Who Burned Columbia?," *The American Historical Review* 7 (April 1902): 485–93; John M. Gibson, *Those 163 Days; a Southern Account of Sherman's March from Atlanta to Raleigh* (New York: Coward-McCann, 1961); John Gilchrist Barrett, *Sherman's March through the Carolinas* (Chapel Hill: University of North Carolina Press, 1956); Marion Brunson Lucas, *Sherman and the Burning of Columbia* (College Station: Texas A & M University Press, 1976); Theodore Rosengarten, "New Views on the Burning of Columbia," *University South Caroliniana Society: Fifty Sixth Annual Meeting*, 1993; Anne Sarah Rubin, *Through the Heart of Dixie: Sherman's March and American Memory* (Chapel Hill: University of North Carolina Press, 2014). A classic Confederate version can be found in William Gilmore Simms and David Aiken, *A City Laid Waste: The Capture, Sack, and Destruction of the City of Columbia* (Columbia: University of South Carolina Press, 2005).

2. Probably Joseph McGath, a private in Company A of the 27th Ohio Infantry. *Index to Compiled Service Records of Volunteer Union Soldiers Who Served in Organizations from the State of Ohio.*

Chapter 32

1. Hampton's plantation Millwood was burned and never rebuilt. Megan Kate Nelson, *Ruin Nation: Destruction and the American Civil War* (Athens: University of Georgia Press, 2012), 70.

2. This is much slower than the March's usual speed of approximately ten miles per day.

3. Marchers frequently swapped horses with Southern civilians. They also killed horses, so the civilians would be left without. See Rubin, *Through the Heart of Dixie*, 51–52.

4. Quimby is referring to his Federal pension. Interestingly, his wound does not appear in his Compiled Service Record. Quimby's first pension application is dated April 30, 1880, and in it he references his wound, and continues to do so in subsequent applications. By 1896, when he was fifty-three, he described himself as "in general decay" and "wholly unable to earn a support by manual labor" because he suffered from sciatic rheumatism, piles, quinsy, catarrh, and severe bronchitis, as well as his gunshot wound. Despite these ailments, Quimby would live another thirty years, though in increasingly frail condition.

Chapter 33

1. This was a common issue with wounds from minie balls, and resulted in rampant infections and gangrene. Quimby was lucky to have the detritus removed from his wound.

2. Quimby appears to be referring to a bizarre tale that circulated in the 1880s. A beautiful Southern woman, who was indeed in Columbia during the burning, left a trail of broken marriages and scandals across Europe and Asia. Her final dalliance, with the prime minister of Japan, resulted in her being executed in 1884 by the Mikado. The entire story can be found in "Beautiful Mrs. Beecher's Career," *The Chicago Tribune*, November 22, 1891. http://archives.chicagotribune.com/1891/11/22/page/7/article/beautiful-mrs-beechers-career#text

Chapter 34

1. Charleston's defenders evacuated the city on February 18, putting it firmly into Union control. James M. McPherson, *Battle Cry of Freedom: The Civil War Era* (New York: Oxford University Press, 1988), 828–29.

2. "Special Field Orders No. 48," *OR*, Series 1, Vol. 47, Part 2, 547–48.

3. Captain Duncan's report (dated February 28, 1865) can be found in *OR*, Series 1, Vol. 47, Part 2, 608–9; it is also mentioned in General Howard's Official Report, April 1, 1865, *OR*, Series 1, Vol. 47, Part 1, 201.

Chapter 35

1. It's unclear to whom Quimby is referring.

2. This appears to be a sarcastic reference to complaints about the rising number and cost of Civil War pensions after 1890. Stuart McConnell, *Glorious Contentment: The Grand Army of the Republic, 1865–1900* (Chapel Hill: University of North Carolina Press, 1992), 143–65; James Alan. Marten, *Sing Not War: The Lives of Union and Confederate Veterans in Gilded Age America* (Chapel Hill: University of North Carolina Press, 2011), 213–19.

Chapter 36

1. Possibly Longtown, SC.

Chapter 37

1. Sherman's army spent several days at Cheraw. Their stay there was notable for the explosion of a vast quantity of Confederate ordnance. While Sherman initially blamed the explosion on Confederate saboteurs, it was, in fact, the fault of a Union soldier. For a detailed look, see Larry E. Nelson, "Sherman at Cheraw," *The South Carolina Historical Magazine, Vol.* 100 (1999): 328–54.

Chapter 38

1. General Alfred H. Terry, who led the Union effort that captured Fort Fisher on January 13, 1865.

2. This is the best documented of Quimby's adventures in Georgia and the Carolinas. In addition to the brief mention in Sherman's *Memoirs*, it is described in greater detail in General O. O. Howard's Official Report and in his *Autobiography*. In both instances, Howard mentions Amick and Quimby by name. William T. Sherman, *Memoirs of General William T. Sherman* (Bloomington: Indiana University Press, 1957), 293; *OR*, Series 1, Vol. 47, Part 1, 203; *OR*, Series 1, Vol. 47, Part 2, 735; O. O. Howard, *Autobiography of Oliver Otis Howard, Major General, United States Army* (New York: Baker & Taylor Co., 1907), Vol. 2, 139.

3. Corporal James Pike detailed his own adventures in his book, *The Scout and Ranger*. He got lost and arrived after Amick and Quimby. James Pike, *The Scout and Ranger: Being the Personal Adventures of Corporal Pike, of the Fourth Ohio Cavalry. As a Texan Ranger, in the Indian Wars, Delineating Western Adventure; Afterwards a Scout and Spy, in Tennessee, Alabama, Georgia, and the Carolinas, under General Mitchell, Rosecrans, Stanley, Sheridan, Lytle, Thomas, Crook, and Sherman. Fully Illustrating the Secret Service. Twenty-Five Full-Page Engravings* (Cincinnati and New York, J. R. Hawley & Co., 1865), 383, 397.

4. "Marching Through Georgia, by General O. O. Howard," *The National Tribune*, March 12, 1896. Howard's wording is essentially the same as he used in his later

Autobiography. O. O. Howard, *Autobiography of Oliver Otis Howard, Major General, United States Army* (New York: Baker & Taylor Co., 1907), Vol. 2, 139.

5. Charles H. Howard, Military Order of the Loyal Legion of the United States, and Commandery of the State of Illinois, *Incidents and Operations Connected with the Capture of Savannah* (Chicago: Cozzens & Beaton Co., 1891).

Chapter 41

1. This unnamed North Carolinian most likely took his oath of allegiance to the Union under the auspices of Lincoln's 1863 Proclamation of Amnesty and Reconstruction, otherwise known as the Ten Percent Plan. This form of wartime reunification called for a state to return to the Union when ten percent of its 1860 voters had taken an oath of future allegiance to the United States. William Alan Blair, *With Malice toward Some: Treason and Loyalty in the Civil War Era*, The Littlefield History of the Civil War Era (Chapel Hill: University of North Carolina Press, 2014), 91. For much more detail, see Harold Melvin Hyman, *Era of the Oath; Northern Loyalty Tests during the Civil War and Reconstruction* (Philadelphia, University of Pennsylvania Press, 1954).

Chapter 42

1. This was a perennial stereotype: that the Eastern Armies were characterized by a stiff formality, while the Western ones were looser, and implicitly for Quimby, better.

2. Quimby is referring to the stories of Jefferson Davis being captured by Union soldiers on May 10, 1865, while wearing his wife's shawl. This story was often exaggerated to feature Davis in full woman's regalia, as way to humiliate both the Confederate president, and his erstwhile nation. See Nina Silber, *The Romance of Reunion: Northerners and the South, 1865–1900*, Civil War America (Chapel Hill: University of North Carolina Press, 1993), 13–38.

3. General Terry's response to General Sherman can be found in *OR*, Series 1, Vol. 47, Part 2, 790. In addition to being mentioned in newspapers, the story of Quimby and Amick's adventures became known to Sherman's men. Thomas Ward Osborn, an artillery officer, wrote in his diary on March 9 that "Gen. Sherman sent Sergeant Emmick of Duncan's Co. to Wilmington with dispatches. He is well versed in the mysteries of scouting. He goes dressed as a Rebel lieutenant." Three days later Osborn noted that Amick's mission had been successful (he made no mention of Quimby) and marveled at Amick's cleverness in hiding the dispatch in a plug of tobacco. Thomas Ward Osborn, Richard Barksdale Harwell, and Philip N. Racine, *The Fiery Trail: A Union Officer's Account of Sherman's Last Campaigns* (Knoxville: University of Tennessee Press, 1986), 172, 179–80.

4. S. M. H. Byers wrote the song, which was once as famous as "Marching Through Georgia," while in a Confederate prison. He escaped during the confusion of the burning of Columbia and made his way to Sherman's headquarters. See Rubin, *Through*

the Heart of Dixie: Sherman's March and American Memory (Chapel Hill: University of North Carolina Press, 2014), 175–79.

Chapter 43

1. General Howard told the story of what happened to Duncan in a letter to Sherman on March 17. Thomas Osborn also includes Duncan's capture and escape in his diary. *OR*, Series 1, Volume 47, Part 2, 870; Osborn, *The Fiery Trail*, 189–90.

2. Quimby appears to be referring to one of the most notorious incidents along the March in South Carolina where two dozen Union foragers were found slaughtered, with "death to all foragers" written on their bodies. Angrily, Sherman wrote to Confederate General Wade Hampton, informing him that "I have ordered a similar number of prisoners in our hand to be disposed of in like manner." Hampton, equally irate, warned Sherman that he would then kill two Union prisoners for every Confederate "murdered." The total number of prisoners killed by either side is unclear, but potentially in the hundreds. Certainly the fear of being captured and killed was both real and ever-present for Quimby and his fellow scouts. Kate Winkler Dawson, "Shannon's Scouts vs. Sherman's Armies," *The New York Times* Disunion Blog, January 21, 2015. http://opinionator.blogs.nytimes.com/2015/01/21/shannons-scouts-vs-shermans-armies/.

3. Quimby decided to hold out for the regular service. On June 14, 1865, he was discharged from the 32nd Wisconsin, and a few days later commissioned as a second lieutenant in the 128th US Colored Troops.

BIBLIOGRAPHY

Primary Sources

Dodge, Grenville Mellen, and Military Order of the Loyal Legion of the United States. New York Commmandery. *Sketch of the Military Service of Major General Wager Swayne.* New York, 1903. http://archive.org/details/sketchofmilitaryoododg.

Dyer, Frederick, ed. *A Compendium of the War of the Rebellion: Compiled and Arranged from Official Records of the Federal and Confederate Armies, Reports of the Adjutant Generals of the Several States, the Army Registers, and Other Reliable Documents and Sources.* Vol. 3. https://archive.org/details/08697590.3359.emory.edu.

Howard, Charles H., Military Order of the Loyal Legion of the United States, and Commandery of the State of Illinois. *Incidents and Operations Connected with the Capture of Savannah.* Chicago: Cozzens & Beaton Company, 1891.

Howard, O. O. *Autobiography of Oliver Otis Howard, Major General, United States Army.* New York: Baker & Taylor Co., 1907.

Nichols, George Ward. *The Story of the Great March.* New York: Harper & Brothers, 1865.

Norton, John, and Nancy Jane Calenberg. *The Norton Civil War Letters.* Baltimore: Publish America, 2004.

Osborn, Thomas Ward, Richard Barksdale Harwell, and Philip N. Racine. *The Fiery Trail: A Union Officer's Account of Sherman's Last Campaigns.* Knoxville: University of Tennessee Press, 1986.

Pike, James. *The Scout and Ranger: Being the Personal Adventures of Corporal Pike, of the Fourth Ohio Cavalry. As a Texan Ranger, in the Indian Wars, Delineating Western Adventure; Afterwards a Scout and Spy, in Tennessee, Alabama, Georgia, and the Carolinas, under General Mitchell, Rosecrans, Stanley, Sheridan, Lytle, Thomas, Crook, and Sherman. Fully Illustrating the Secret Service. Twenty-Five Full-Page Engravings.* Cincinnati and New York: J.R. Hawley & Co., 1865. http://archive.org/details/scoutrangerbeingoopike.

Quiner, E[dwin] B[entley]. *The Military History of Wisconsin: A Record of the Civil and Military Patriotism of the State, in the War for the Union, with a History of the Campaigns in Which Wisconsin Soldiers Have Been Conspicuous—Regimental Histories— Sketches of Distinguished Officers—the Roll of the Illustrious Dead—Movements of the Legislature and State Officers, Etc.* Chicago: Clarke & Co., 1866. https://archive.org/details/militaryhistoryoooquin.

Sherman, William T. *Memoirs of General William T. Sherman.* Bloomington: Indiana University Press, 1957.

Simms, William Gilmore, and David Aiken. *A City Laid Waste: The Capture, Sack, and Destruction of the City of Columbia.* Columbia: University of South Carolina Press, 2005.

Simpson, Brooks D., and Jean V. Berlin, eds. *Sherman's Civil War: Selected Correspondence of William T. Sherman, 1860–1865*. Chapel Hill: University of North Carolina Press, 1999.

Society of the Army of the Tennessee, "Report of the Proceedings of the Annual Meeting of the Society of the Army of the Tennessee," 1869.

United States War Department, Robert N. Scott, H. M. Lazelle, George B. Davis, Leslie J. Perry, Joseph W. Kirkley, et al. *The War of the Rebellion: A Compilation of the Official Records of the Union and Confederate Armies*. Washington, DC: Government Printing Office, 1880.

Wills, Charles Wright, and Mary E. Kellogg. *Army Life of an Illinois Soldier: Including a Day-by-Day Record of Sherman's March to the Sea: Letters and Diary of Charles W. Wills*. Shawnee classics. Carbondale: Southern Illinois University Press, 1996.

Wood, Alanson. *History of the 32nd Regiment, Wisconsin Infantry*, n.d.

Secondary Sources

Bailey, Anne J. *War and Ruin: William T. Sherman and the Savannah Campaign*. Wilmington: Scholarly Resources, 2003.

Barrett, John Gilchrist. *Sherman's March through the Carolinas*. Chapel Hill: University of North Carolina Press, 1956.

Beymer, William Gilmore. *Scouts and Spies of the Civil War*. Lincoln: University of Nebraska Press, 2003.

Blair, William Alan. *With Malice toward Some: Treason and Loyalty in the Civil War Era*. The Littlefield History of the Civil War Era. Chapel Hill: University of North Carolina Press, 2014.

Blight, David W. *Race and Reunion: The Civil War in American Memory*. Cambridge, Mass.: Belknap Press of Harvard University Press, 2001.

Bonner, James C. *Milledgeville: Georgia's Antebelleum Capital*. Athens: University of Georgia Press, 1978.

Bradley, Mark L. *Last Stand in the Carolinas: The Battle of Bentonville*. Campbell, Calif.: Savas Publishers, 1996.

Bradley, Mark L. *This Astounding Close: The Road to the Bennett Place*. Chapel Hill: University of North Carolina Press, 2000.

Broadwater, Robert P. *Battle of Despair: Bentonville and the North Carolina Campaign*. Macon, Ga.: Mercer University Press, 2004.

Broadwater, Robert P. *Civil War Special Forces: The Elite and Distinct Fighting Units of the Union and Confederate Armies*. Santa Barbara: Praeger, 2014.

Browning, Robert M. *Success Is All That Was Expected: The South Atlantic Blockading Squadron during the Civil War*. Washington, DC: Brassey's, Inc., 2002.

Campbell, Jacqueline Glass. *When Sherman Marched North from the Sea*. Chapel Hill: University of North Carolina Press, 2003.

Central Intelligence Agency, "Intelligence in the Civil War," n.d.

Davis, Curtis Carroll. "Companions of Crisis: The Spy Memoir as a Social Document." *Civil War History, Vol.* 10, No. 4 (n.d.): 385–400.

Davis, Stephen. *What the Yankees Did to Us: Sherman's Bombardment and Wrecking of Atlanta.* Macon, Ga.: Mercer University Press, 2012.

Derden, John K. *The World's Largest Prison: The Story of Camp Lawton.* Macon, Ga.: Mercer University Press, 2012.

Durham, Roger S. *Guardian of Savannah: Fort McAllister, Georgia, in the Civil War and beyond. Studies in Maritime History.* Columbia, SC: University of South Carolina Press, 2008.

Fishel, Edwin C. "The Mythology of Civil War Intelligence." *Civil War History,* Vol. 10, No. 4 (n.d.): 344–67.

Fishel, Edwin C. *The Secret War for the Union: The Untold Story of Military Intelligence in the Civil War,* 1996.

Frank, Lisa Tendrich. *The Civilian War: Confederate Women and Union Soldiers during Sherman's March.* Baton Rouge: Louisiana State University Press, 2015.

Gibson, John M. *Those 163 Days; a Southern Account of Sherman's March from Atlanta to Raleigh.* New York: Coward-McCann, 1961.

Glatthaar, Joseph T. *The March to the Sea and Beyond.* Baton Rouge: Louisiana State University Press, 1985.

Harrington, Hugh T. *Civil War Milledgeville: Tales from the Confederate Capital of Georgia.* Charleston: History Press, 2005.

Hyman, Harold Melvin. *Era of the Oath; Northern Loyalty Tests during the Civil War and Reconstruction.* Philadelphia, University of Pennsylvania Press, 1954.

Janney, Caroline E. *Remembering the Civil War: Reunion and the Limits of Reconciliation.* Chapel Hill: University of North Carolina Press, 2013.

Jones, Jacqueline. *Saving Savannah: The City and the Civil War.* New York: Alfred A. Knopf, 2008.

Jordan, Brian Matthew. *Marching Home: Union Veterans and Their Unending Civil War.* New York: Liveright Publishing Corporation, a division of W. W. Norton & Company, 2014.

Lucas, Marion Brunson. *Sherman and the Burning of Columbia.* College Station: Texas A & M University Press, 1976.

McConnell, Stuart. *Glorious Contentment: The Grand Army of the Republic, 1865–1900.* Chapel Hill: University of North Carolina Press, 1992.

McPherson, James M. *Battle Cry of Freedom: The Civil War Era.* New York: Oxford University Press, 2003.

Olson, Gordon L. *The Notorious Isaac Earl and His Scouts: Union Soldiers, Prisoners, Spies,* 2014.

Roth, Lottie Roeder. *History of Whatcom County.* Vol. II. Chicago: Pioneer Historical Pub. Co., 1926.

Rubin, Anne Sarah. *Through the Heart of Dixie: Sherman's March and American Memory*, 2014.

Stephenson, Darl L. *Headquarters in the Brush: Blazer's Independent Union Scouts*. Athens: Ohio University Press, 2001.

Trudeau, Noah Andre. *Southern Storm: Sherman's March to the Sea*. New York: Harper, 2008.

Venet, Wendy Hammond. *A Changing Wind: Commerce & Conflict in Civil War Atlanta*. New Haven: Yale University Press, 2014.

INDEX

South Edisto River, SC, 104, 110
Southern whites, 9, 19–20, 36–37, 38, 59,
     86–89, 100–102, 105–106, 126, 128, 132,
     135–138, 146, 154–55
Special Field Orders No. 120, xi, xvii
Stevenson, [George], 20, 82, 86–89
Stokesbury, 19–20, 87–88

Taylor, Jim, 7, 47
Terry, Alfred, 142, 145, 158
Texas Rangers, 31–32, 34–35
32nd Wisconsin Infantry, xiii–xv, xix, 40,
     99, 161
Thomas, George, 5, 27
20th Corps, xvi
29th Missouri Mounted Infantry, 39–40,
     46–47

USS Bellerophon. See *USS Flag*
USS Dandelion, 70–71, 74–77
USS Flag, 68
USS Philadelphia, 70–78
USS Silver Moon, 71

veterans, xii, 134

Wallace, Pat, 7, 34–37, 44–47, 86, 129–131,
     136, 162
Wheeler, Joseph, xvii, 8, 57
Wheeler's Confederate cavalry, 8–10, 43,
     57–58, 88
White, John A., xiii–xiv, 40, 86, 94, 131,
     136, 140, 162
Williams, Alpheus, C., xvi
Wood, Charles R., 111